SPA

To stay informed about upcoming TASCHEN titles, please request our magazine at

www.taschen.com/magazine or write to TASCHEN, Hohenzollernring 53, D-50672 Cologne, Germany,

contact@taschen.com, Fax: +49-221-254919. We will be happy to send you a free copy of our magazine

which is filled with information about all of our books.

Hohenzollernring 53, D–50672 Köln

www.taschen.com

Concept and idea by: Angelika Taschen, Berlin

Edited by: Allison Arieff, San Francisco

Design: Bryan Burkhart/MODERNHOUSE, San Francisco

Cover design: Sense/Net, Andy Disl and Birgit Reber, Cologne

Text by: Allison Arieff, Adrienne Arieff, Deborah Bishop, Irene Ricasio Edwards, San Francisco

Project management: Viola Krauß, Kathrin Murr, Cologne

Production: Horst Neuzner, Cologne

German translation: Christiane Burkhardt, textkontor, Munich

French translation: Marie Surgers, Hélène Marin and Arnaud Briand for mot.tiff, Paris

Printed in China

ISBN 978-3-8365-0190-3

SPA

ANGELIKA TASCHEN

ALLISON ARIEFF and **BRYAN BURKHART**

with **ADRIENNE ARIEFF** / **DEBORAH BISHOP** / **IRENE RICASIO EDWARDS**

TASCHEN

HONG KONG KÖLN LONDON LOS ANGELES MADRID PARIS TOKYO

Asia

Africa & Middle East

Caribbean

Europe

North America

Mexico &
South America

Oceania

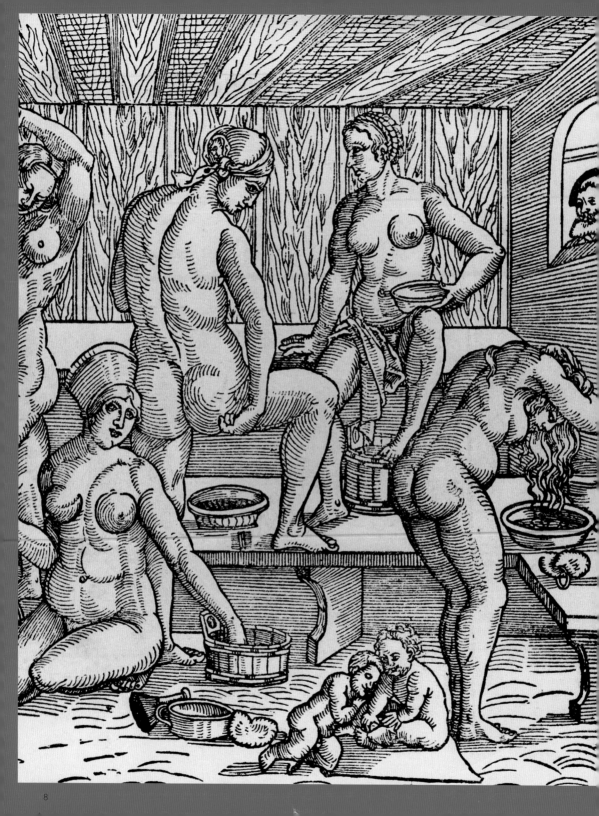

Introduction

When in doubt, take a bath

—MAE WEST

For most of us, the spa experience occurs mostly at home, in the tub. There are bubbles, maybe even candles, and – hopefully – there is peace and quiet. As pleasurable as these 30- or 40-minute diversions can be, however, they pale in comparison to the total escape that comes with a visit to a spa. It may take you 24 hours, even 36, to forget the traffic, the bills, the office – in short, all the quotidian elements that characterize your life in the real world. But once you have surrendered to all that your spa destination has to offer – massages that erase those daily concerns, contemplative walks (or vigorous hikes) at sunrise, the delicious strain of a well-taught yoga session, a decadent hour spent lingering over breakfast, the simple delight of dipping one's toe in pool or ocean – you will never be fully content with the tub again. The gorgeous properties featured herein, from Milan to Maui, Stockholm to San Francisco, go above and beyond the standard fare of Swedish massage and steam room, offering instead a dazzling array of treatments, recreational activities, and accommodation. Indeed, it is possible to schedule a day consisting of whale watching, cookery class, and reflexology. So turn the page now and discover where you want to go …

Bei den meisten beschränkt sich die Spa-Erfahrung auf die heimische Badewanne. Das Wasser sprudelt, vielleicht brennen ein paar Kerzen und wenn man Glück hat, herrschen Ruhe und Frieden. So schön diese 30–40-minütigen Auszeiten auch sein mögen, verblassen sie doch völlig im Vergleich zu einem echten Spa-Erlebnis. Manchmal dauert es 24, ja sogar 36 Stunden, bis man den Verkehr, die Rechnungen, das Büro hinter sich gelassen hat – kurz, unseren ganz normalen Alltag. Aber wenn man sich erst einmal auf das einlässt, was so ein Spa zu bieten hat – Massagen, die einen alle Sorgen vergessen lassen, beschauliche Spaziergänge (oder flotte Wanderungen) bei Tagesanbruch, die wohlige Dehnung, die eine gute Yoga-Stunde bringt, ein ausgiebiges Frühstück von nicht unter einer Stunde, den Genuss, den großen Zeh in den Pool oder das Meer zu tauchen – wird man sich nicht mehr so schnell mit der heimischen Badewanne zufrieden geben. Die in diesem Buch gezeigten herrlichen Spa-Resorts von Mailand bis Maui, von Stockholm bis San Francisco, warten nicht nur mit einer klassischen schwedischen Massage oder einem Dampfbad auf, sondern bieten eine geradezu Schwindel erregende Auswahl an Anwendungen, Erholungsaktivitäten sowie ein Ambiente für jeden Geschmack. Ein Tag mit Whale Watching, dem Besuch eines Kochkurses und einer Reflexologie-Behandlung liegt also durchaus im Bereich des Möglichen. Worauf warten Sie? Blättern Sie um und gehen Sie auf Entdeckungsreise …

Bien souvent, l'expérience du spa se résume à se prélasser dans sa baignoire: beaucoup de mousse, quelques bougies et un peu de calme et de tranquillité. Certes très agréables, ces moments de détente ne durent généralement guère plus d'une demi-heure et ne peuvent rivaliser avec l'évasion totale qu'offre un établissement spécialisé. Une journée ou deux pourront être nécessaires pour oublier tous les tracas de la vie quotidienne – les embouteillages, les factures, le travail … Mais après avoir succombé aux charmes du spa de vos rêves – massages relaxants, promenades méditatives (ou randonnées sportives) au lever du jour, plaisirs revigorants d'une séance de yoga, douceur d'un petit déjeuner qui s'éternise, bonheur de tremper ses orteils dans la piscine ou l'océan –, vous ne regarderez plus jamais votre baignoire comme avant! De Milan à Maui, de Stockholm à San Francisco, les somptueux établissements présentés dans cet ouvrage offrent bien plus que les traditionnelles étuves et les classiques massages suédois. Ils vous proposent un éventail impressionnant de soins, d'activités de loisirs et de prestations hôtelières. Que diriez-vous d'une journée passée à observer les baleines, à prendre des cours de cuisine et de réflexologie? Tournez la page et choisissez votre destination …

– ALLISON ARIEFF

9

Africa & Middle East

Mövenpick Resort & Spa Dead Sea

The Mövenpick Resort & Spa of the Dead Sea is the latest of 44 hotels owned by Mövenpick. The Dead Sea location focuses on its most unique asset – the high salt concentration of the water, said to contain healing properties. Accordingly, the Mövenpick offers activities such as mud and flotation rejuvenation, and yoga-balance sessions, meditation and relaxation rituals at the Dead Sea shore. As for spa treatments, Mövenpick & Dead Sea houses the Sanctuary Zara Spa, run by the UK's Sanctuary Spa Group. The visuals of the Sanctuary Zara Spa are traditional Arab architecture contrasting with modern features like the terrace pool, with its infinity edge looking onto the Dead Sea. Also popular are the spa's thermariums, each providing a hot dry room, a warm steam room, soap massage room, and tropical rain showers. The spa also provides four mud therapy rooms and several hydrotherapy suites, with dry flotation baths, shower massages, and hydrotherapy massage baths. The spa's\tranquility room" has views of the sea from the room's arched windows and veranda. More conventional spa treatments include a manicure and pedicure room and facials. The spa, as well as the rest of the 340-room resort, emphasizes its indoor/outdoor environment.

SIGNATURE TREATMENT: THERMARIUMS

Das Mövenpick Resort & Spa am Toten Meer ist das neueste der 44 Hotels, die zur Mövenpick-Kette gehören. Aufgrund seiner Lage dreht sich hier alles um das stark salzhaltige Meerwasser, dem große Heilwirkung zugeschrieben wird. Dementsprechend bietet das Mövenpick unter anderem Anwendungen wie die Schlamm- und „Flotation"-Verjüngungskur an. Yoga, Meditation und andere Entspannungstechniken werden ebenfalls direkt am Toten Meer praktiziert. Weitere Wellnessbehandlungen bietet das hauseigene Sanctuary Zara Spa, das zur britischen Sanctuary Spa Group gehört. Das im arabischen Stil errichtete Spa steht in einem reizvollen Kontrast zu seiner hochmodernen Ausstattung, zu der unter anderem ein Terrassenpool mit Blick aufs Tote Meer gehört. Großer Beliebtheit erfreuen sich auch die Thermarien des Spa mit Sauna, Dampfbad, Massageraum und Tropenregen-Duschen. Für Schlammbehandlungen stehen vier Räume zur Verfügung, an die sich mehrere Hydrotherapie-Suiten anschließen. „Dry-Flotation"- und diverse Massagebäder runden das Angebot ab. Vom Ruheraum mit seinen Bogenfenstern und der vorgelagerten Terrasse hat man einen herrlichen Blick aufs Meer. Zu den konventionelleren Wellnessanwendungen gehören Maniküre, Pediküre und Kosmetikbehandlungen. Der Wellnessbereich wie auch das 340-Betten-Hotel fügen sich nahtlos in die malerische Umgebung ein.

WELLNESS-SPECIAL: THERMARIEN

Situé sur les rives de la mer Morte, le Mövenpick Resort & Spa est le dernier-né des 44 hôtels Mövenpick. Il tire avantage de l'eau de la mer Morte, très salée et reconnue pour ses vertus curatives. Le Mövenpick offre des activités telles que traitements régénérants à base de boue, bain flottant, yoga, méditation, relaxation, sur les rivages de la mer Morte. Le Sanctuary Zara Spa, qui dépend du groupe britannique Sanctuary Spa Group, combine l'architecture arabe traditionnelle à des éléments modernes comme la piscine découverte à débordement, qui semble se jeter dans la mer Morte. À ne pas manquer non plus, les thermariums : une salle de chaleur sèche, une salle de bains à vapeur, une salle de massage et des douches tropicales parfumées à la menthe. Quatre pièces sont réservées aux soins à base de boue, d'autres à l'hydrothérapie avec des bains flottants à sec, des douches massantes et des bains à jets directionnels. Les fenêtres voûtées et la véranda de la salle de relaxation ont vue sur la mer. Des traitments plus conventionels comme la manucure, pédicure et les soins du visage sont également proposés. Le complexe thermal, qui compte 340 chambres, joue sur l'union de l'intérieur et de l'extérieur.

SOIN PHARE : THERMARIUMS

Mövenpick Resort & Spa Dead Sea
Dead Sea Road, Sweimeh
11180 Amman, Jordan

TEL: +962 5 3561111
FAX: +962 5 3561122
EMAIL: resort.deadsea@moevenpick.com
WEBSITE: www.moevenpick-deadsea.com

Amanjena Resort & Spa

Amanjena, Moroccan for "peaceful paradise," is an oasis in the middle of Morocco's sandy dunes and dry desert winds. The resort's monumental pools serve as tranquil focal points, surrounded by authentic glazed Moroccan tiling and sandy clay roofs. The spa's 28 pavilions and six two-story "maisons" are located in a fertile patch of palms and mature olive trees. The rose-blush walls of Amanjena echo the city walls of Marrakesh, which is known as the Red City. Its buildings are based on the historical designs of ancient Moorish pisé (packed earth) structures, as well as the Berber villages that cling to the region's nearby High Atlas Mountains. Water is the unifying element of Amanjena, which has at its center a large basin, traditionally a holding pool to collect water for irrigation. Amanjena's spa prides itself on its hammam, a steam bath with traditional exfoliation treatments. The spa also has a separate sauna and steam room. Services include a range of massage and alternative therapies, facials, scrubs, body wraps, baths, and beauty treatments. If you want to tone your body as well as relax, Amajena's timber-floor gym provides a perfect place to sweat it out.

SIGNATURE TREATMENT: STEAM BATHS

Amanjena, marokkanisch für „friedliches Paradies", ist eine Oase inmitten von Marokkos Sanddünen, über die ein heißer, trockener Wind streicht. Die riesigen Pools der Anlage, gesäumt von traditionellen marokkanischen Fliesen und Lehmbauten, sind ein echter Blickfang. Die 28 Pavillons und sechs zweistöckigen *maisons* des Spa liegen auf fruchtbarem Boden, umgeben von Palmen und alten Olivenbäumen. Die rosaroten Wände von Amanjena erinnern an die Stadtmauern von Marrakesch, das auch „Die Rote Stadt" genannt wird. Die gesamte Anlage wurde im Stil der alten maurischen Lehmarchitektur errichtet, wie man sie auch in den Berberdörfern sehen kann, die an den nahe gelegenen Hängen des Hohen Atlas kleben. Wasser ist das hervorstechendste Element in Amanjena. In der Mitte der Anlage befindet sich ein riesiges Becken, das nach marokkanischer Tradition ursprünglich ein Sammelbecken zur Bewässerung war. Besonders stolz ist das Spa auf sein Hamam (Dampfbad) mit traditionellen Peelings. Außerdem verfügt es über eine separate Sauna. Das Spa bietet eine große Auswahl an Massagen und anderen Wellness-Therapien. Dazu gehören Gesichtsbehandlungen ebenso wie Peelings, Bodywraps, Bäder sowie diverse Schönheitsanwendungen. Wer etwas für seine Figur tun möchte, kann sich im hauseigenen Studio mit Holzboden austoben.

WELLNESS-SPECIAL: DAMPFBÄDER

Amanjena, qui signifie « paradis paisible » en marocain, est une oasis au milieu de dunes de sable caressées par les vents du désert. L'hôtel, avec son carrelage en authentique céramique marocaine et ses toits d'argile clair, s'organise autour de vastes bassins. Les 28 bungalows et les six « pavillons » à deux étages sont entourés de palmiers et d'oliviers centenaires. La couleur des murs est en harmonie avec ceux de Marrakech, souvent nommée la « ville rouge ». L'architecture s'inspire des bâtiments en pisé des anciens Maures et des villages berbères des contreforts de l'Atlas. L'élément Eau est omniprésent à Amanjena, dont le patio central sert d'écrin à un immense bassin semblable à ceux utilisés traditionnellement pour l'irrigation. Le hammam, un bain de vapeur traditionnel associé à des soins exfoliants, fait la fierté du spa d'Amanjena, mais l'établissement dispose également d'un sauna et de plusieurs salles de vapeur. Les soins proposés comprennent différents types de massage, des traitements alternatifs, des masques, des gommages, des enveloppements, des bains et des soins esthétiques. Amanjena conjugue forme et détente grâce à une salle de gym.

SOIN PHARE : BAINS DE VAPEUR

Amanjena Resort & Spa
Route de Ouarzazate, Km 12
Marrakesh, Morocco

TEL: +212 24 403 353
FAX: +212 24 403 477
EMAIL: amanjena@amanresorts.com
WEBSITE: www.amanresorts.com

The Chedi

Lush palm gardens, elegant vanishing-edge pools, contemporary minimalist Omani architecture, and seemingly endless stretches of private beach with views of the Gulf of Oman and the gorgeous mountain ranges of Muscat, make The Chedi a top-destination resort. Surrounded by the sparkling blue waters of the Indian Ocean, The Chedi takes a cue from the lavish lifestyle of His Majesty the Sultan, and pampers its lucky guests with luxurious rooms, fantasy-inducing gardens and pools, and a world-class restaurant. In the 161 modern rooms and private villas in this five-star beach resort, the decor is exquisite and every indulgence is provided, from sunken tubs to luxurious high-thread-count linens to glorious views of either the ocean or the mountains of Muscat. In The Chedi's elegantly appointed spa, treatments offered include traditional Thai massage; oil-free, energy-freeing Japanese massage, and tension-relieving Balinese massage. The 90-minute signature Chedi Massage is a blend of aromatherapy and Western spa techniques: full hand strokes move rhythmically from head to feet in an unpredictable, relaxing flow. A special foot massage incorporates Mediterranean essences of juniper and tangerine to cleanse and rejuvenate the feet through reflexology.

SIGNATURE TREATMENT: THE CHEDI MASSAGE

Üppige Palmengärten, elegante Naturpools, eine modern-minimalistische, landestypische Architektur sowie ein schier endloser Privatstrand mit Blick auf den Golf von Oman und die beeindruckende Gebirgskette von Maskat machen das Chedi zu einem erstklassigen Hotel. Umgeben vom türkisblauen Indischen Ozean, orientiert man sich hier am verschwenderischen Lebensstil Seiner Majestät des Sultans und verwöhnt seine glücklichen Gäste mit luxuriösen Zimmern, fantasievollen Gärten, diversen Pools und einem Restaurant der Spitzenklasse. Alle 161 Zimmer und Privatvillen der Fünf-Sterne-Anlage sind exquisit eingerichtet und bieten jeden nur erdenklichen Komfort – von eingelassenen Wannen über dicht gewebtes Leinen bis hin zu einer herrlichen Aussicht auf den Ozean oder die Berge von Maskat. Das hauseigene, elegante Spa bietet unter anderem Anwendungen wie die traditionelle Thai-Massage, eine belebende Japanische Trockenmassage und die entspannende Bali-Massage an: Das Wellness-Special, die 90-minütige Chedi-Massage, ist eine Mischung aus Aromatherapie und westlichen Spa-Anwendungen. Dabei wird man von Kopf bis Fuß durchgeknetet, bis man alles um sich herum vergisst. Bei einer speziellen Fußmassage kommen mediterrane Wacholder- und Mandarinenessenzen zum Einsatz, um die Füße zu reinigen und mithilfe der Reflexologie zu verjüngen.

WELLNESS-SPECIAL: CHEDI-MASSAGE

Palmeraies luxuriantes, élégantes piscines à débordement, architecture minimaliste typiquement contemporaine, plages privées s'étendant à perte de vue vers le golfe d'Oman et les montagnes majestueuses dominant Mascate : le Chedi Muscat est une destination de rêve. Face aux eaux cristallines de l'Océan indien, le Chedi s'inspire du mode de vie somptueux de sa Majesté le sultan, et offre à ses hôtes une vie de privilégiés : chambres luxueuses, piscines et jardins enchanteurs, restaurant de haute gastronomie. Les 161 chambres et villas privées de ce complexe cinq-étoiles à la décoration exquise sont dotées de tous les luxes : baignoires encastrées, draps fins, vue grandiose sur la mer ou les montagnes de Mascate. Dans le spa lui-même, les soins proposés comprennent massages thaïs traditionnels, massages japonais énergisants, sans huile, et massages balinais relaxants. Son soin phare, le massage Chedi, dure 90 minutes et combine l'aromathérapie aux techniques occidentales ; des pieds à la tête, les pressions rythmées assurent détente et relaxation. Le massage des pieds utilise les propriétés purifiantes et régénérantes des essences de genévrier et de tangerine ainsi que les principes de la réflexologie.

SOIN PHARE : MASSAGE CHEDI

The Chedi
North Ghubra 232
Way No. 3215, Street No. 46
Muscat, Sultanate of Oman

TEL: +968 24 52 44 00
FAX: +968 24 49 34 85
EMAIL: chedimuscat@ghmhotels.com
WEBSITE: www.ghmhotels.com

Asia

Ananda in the Himalayas

Ananda (ancient Sanskrit for "happiness and contentment") in the mystical Himalayas spreads over a hundred acres of undulating forest in South Asia. Seventy-five rooms set amid magnificent gardens are all privy to breathtaking views of the Ganges River and the surrounding hills. Ananda's Wellness Center consists of over 21,000 square feet supremely dedicated to spiritual reawakening and physical rejuvenation, and offers a wide array of yoga and meditation classes and workshops. Intrinsic to Ananda's spa treatments is the natural Himalayan spring water that is used in the sauna, steam room, hot and cold plunge baths, and in the stress-relieving hydrotherapy treatments. Ayurvedic treatments incorporating centuries-old herbal remedies combined with more contemporary Western approaches characterize the Ananda spa's signature offerings. Massage therapies include classic Swedish massage, Thai massage, aromatherapy massage, the stress-relieving Ananda Touch massage, and the intimate Couples massage performed in the spa's Kama Suite. Natural ingredients such as the Detox Papaya Body Polish are used in spa treatments for their natural properties and powers. Beyond the spa walls, guests can also trek, mountain bike, fish for trout or the mighty mahseer (a fish which can measure up to eight feet long), ride the rapids of the Ganges, or even take a safari to catch a glimpse of tigers, elephants, and leopards.

SIGNATURE TREATMENT: AYURVEDIC TREATMENTS

Das Ananda (Sanskrit für „Glück und Zufriedenheit") erstreckt sich über 50 Hektar Wald in Südostasien. 75 inmitten eines prächtigen Parks gelegene Zimmer bieten eine fantastische Aussicht auf den Ganges und die Hügellandschaft der Umgebung. Das 2 000 Quadratmeter große Spa hat sich der Verjüngung von Geist und Körper verschrieben und bietet eine große Auswahl an Yoga- und Meditationskursen sowie Workshops. Charakteristisch für seine Behandlungen ist das original Himalaya-Quellwasser, das bei Sauna, Dampfraum, heißen und kalten Bädern sowie der entspannenden Hydrotherapie zum Einsatz kommt. Für die Wellness-Specials des Ananda werden Ayurveda-Anwendungen mit seit Jahrhunderten bewährten Heilkräutern und moderne Behandlungsformen nach westlichem Vorbild kombiniert. Wer massiert werden will, hat die Wahl zwischen der klassischen Schwedischen Behandlung, der Thai-, der Aromatherapie- und der entspannenden „Ananda-Touch"-Massage. Außerdem wird in der Kama-Suite eine Massage speziell für Paare angeboten. Bei den Spa-Anwendungen wie dem entschlackenden Papaya-Peeling greift man hauptsächlich auf natürliche Zutaten zurück und vertraut der Kraft der Natur. Außerhalb des Spa können die Gäste an Trekking- und Mountain-Bike-Touren teilnehmen, Forellen oder den mächtigen, bis zu 2,5 m langen „Mahseer" angeln, auf dem Ganges raften, ja sogar eine Safari zu Tigern, Elefanten und Leoparden unternehmen.

WELLNESS-SPECIAL: AYURVEDA-BEHANDLUNGEN

Ananda (« bonheur et contentement » en sanskrit), au cœur de l'Himalaya, s'étend sur 50 hectares de forêt. Dans les magnifiques jardins, 75 chambres donnent sur le Gange et les collines environnantes. Le spa, avec ses 2 000 mètres carrés dédiés à la redécouverte de soi et au rajeunissement physique, propose une large gamme de cours et d'ateliers de yoga et de méditation. À la base du programme de soins, l'eau de source de l'Himalaya est utilisée dans le sauna, la salle de vapeur, les bains froids et chauds et les traitements hydrothérapiques anti-stress. La caractéristique du spa Ananda est de combiner les remèdes ayurvédiques à base de plantes connus dequis des siècles avec une approche occidentale moderne. Les massages proposés sont suédois, thaïlandais, aromathérapique, anti-stress (massage Ananda Touch), ou, plus intime, le massage pour couples, effectué dans la suite Kama (« désir », « amour »). Les soins mettent à profit les propriétés d'ingrédients naturels comme la papaye aux vertus détoxifiantes. La nature environnante invite à pratiquer le trekking, le VTT, la pêche à la truite ou au mahseer (qui peut mesurer jusqu'à 2,5 mètres), à descendre les rapides du Gange, ou encore à partir en safari à la découverte des tigres, des éléphants et des léopards.

SOIN PHARE : TRAITEMENTS AYURVÉDIQUES

Ananda in the Himalayas
The Palace Estate
Narendra Nagar, Dist. Tehri-Garhwal
Uttaranchal, 249175, India

TEL: +91 1378 227500
FAX: +91 1378 227550
EMAIL: sales@anandaspa.com
WEBSITE: www.anandaspa.com

COMO Shambhala Estate at Begawan Giri

For centuries, Begawan Giri was known as "Wise Man's Mountain," a 20-acre parcel of serenity hidden amid the emerald hills, rivers, forests, and rice fields of central Bali. Just outside the cultural center of Ubud, the estate with 12 villas and residences fuses Asian and European design influences to dramatic effect. Architect Cheong Yew Kuan created each residence to evoke a unique aspect of Indonesian culture "from a luxury tree house to a maharajah's palace" and filled each with exquisite artifacts, furnishings, and art. (A 24-hour personal butler assigned to each residence fulfills every request.) A steep stone staircase leads to landscaped water gardens fed by mountain springs; next to the Ayung River lies the Source spa, which draws its inspiration from the nearby springs as well as from Bali's healing rituals. Treatments can be performed in outdoor pavilions or in the privacy of the guest's own villa. Choices include the two-hour Mandi Lulur ("royal wedding treatment"), in which a Balinese-style massage is combined with a body mask of rice flour, turmeric, and jasmine, followed by a soak in a flower bath. In keeping with the fundamental spirituality of the region, yoga and energy work are also on hand, along with sessions from visiting masters trained in various forms of healing.

SIGNATURE TREATMENT: MANDI LULUR

Seit Jahrhunderten gilt der Begawan Giri als „Berg des weisen Mannes". Das acht Hektar umfassende Idyll inmitten von smaragdgrünen Hügeln, Flüssen, Wäldern und Reisfeldern liegt im Herzen Balis, in der Nähe des kulturellen Zentrums Ubud gelegen. In der Anlage mit zwölf Villen und Residenzen gehen asiatisches und europäisches Design eine gelungene Verbindung ein. Um die kulturelle Vielfalt Indonesiens zu zeigen, hat der Architekt Cheong Yew Kuan jede Unterkunft unterschiedlich gestaltet: Ob luxuriöses Baumhaus oder prächtiger Maharadscha-Palast – alle wurden mit exquisitem Mobiliar und kostbaren Kunstgegenständen ausgestattet. (Zu jeder Residenz gehört ein rund um die Uhr zur Verfügung stehender Butler, der den Gästen jeden Wunsch erfüllt.) Eine steile Steintreppe führt zu den von Bergquellen gespeisten Wassergärten. Das Spa liegt am Ayung-Fluss und macht sich die nahe gelegenen Quellen ebenso zunutze wie die balinesischen Heilrituale. Anwendungen können in Pavillons oder in der eigenen Villa in Anspruch genommen werden. Dazu gehört auch das zweistündige Mandi Lulur („Königliche Hochzeitsbehandlung"), das eine balinesische Massage sowie eine Körperpackung aus Reismehl, Kurkuma und Jasmin beinhaltet. Den Abschluss bildet ein Bad im Blütenbecken. Im Einklang mit der spirituellen Atmosphäre dieses Ortes werden auch Yoga und Energiearbeit angeboten, wobei erfahrene Meister die Gäste in verschiedene Heilrituale einweisen.

WELLNESS-SPECIAL: MANDI LULUR

Depuis des siècles, Begawan Giri est appelé « la montagne du Sage ». Sans doute parce que la nature y déploie dix hectares de sérénité dans l'émeraude des collines, rivières, forêts et rizières du centre de Bali. Tout proche d'Ubud, le cœur culturel de l'île, les douze villas et résidences opèrent la fusion spectaculaire des influences asiatiques et européennes. Cheong Yew Kuan, l'architecte, a voulu que chaque résidence évoque un aspect de la culture indonésienne, depuis la luxueuse maison-arbre jusqu'au palais d'un maharadjah, et soit décorée de meubles et d'objets d'arts exquis. Dans chacune des résidences, un majordome est présent en permanence pour répondre à tous les désirs de ses hôtes. Un escalier de pierre mène aux bassins des jardins paysagers ; près de l'Ayung, le spa s'inspire à la fois des sources toutes proches et des rituels balinais. Les soins peuvent être prodigués dans les pavillons extérieurs ou dans les villas privatives, comme par exemple le Mandi lulur (« soin du mariage royal »), combinaison d'un massage balinais et d'un masque corporel fait de farine de riz, de safran et de jasmin, suivie d'un bain de fleurs : deux heures de pur bonheur. Comme le veut la spiritualité omniprésente dans la région, le yoga et le travail sur les énergies sont à l'honneur, ainsi que des sessions dirigées par des maîtres invités, spécialistes de diverses disciplines.

SOIN PHARE : MANDI LULUR

COMO Shambhala Estate at Begawan Giri
Ubud 80571
Bali, Indonesia

TEL: +62 361 978888
FAX: +62 361 978889
EMAIL: res@cse.comoshambhala.bz
WEBSITE: cse.comoshambhala.bz

Four Seasons Resort Bali at Sayan

Just ten minutes from the island's cultural and artistic center of Ubud, the Four Seasons Bali at Sayan is an exotic retreat featuring 18 beautifully appointed suites and 42 secluded villas, each with a private plunge pool. All guest accommodations offer impressive views of the verdant Ayung River valley. Sayan boasts three Spa Villas that reflect the elegant Balinese architecture of the resort. Natural materials combine with native designs in such blissful elements as hand-loomed Sulawesi silk furniture coverings, customized terrazzo massage tables, and thatched roofs. The Spa Villas can accommodate tandem treatments for couples, and each is connected to outdoor bathing pavilions offering steam showers. Large soaking tubs with adjacent open-air showers discreetly overlook private garden courtyards. Spicy treatments on offer at the Spa include the red ginger body polish, the basil rosemary body wrap, and the Balinese massage. For the ultimate in relaxation and luxury, try the lavish Lulur Sayan body treatment, a Javanese beauty ritual that begins with an invigorating herbal exfoliation scrub followed by a cooling yogurt splash. The pampering continues with a soothing ylang-ylang petal bath and a relaxing Balinese massage using fragrant mountain-flower body lotion. After body and mind have been rejuvenated, a jamu herbal elixir is served to complete the ritual.

SIGNATURE TREATMENT: LULUR SAYAN BODY TREATMENT

Das nur zehn Minuten vom Künstlerdorf Ubud entfernte Four Seasons Bali at Sayan ist eine exotische Anlage mit 18 prächtig ausgestatteten Suiten und 42 Villen, von denen jede über einen eigenen Pool verfügt. Von allen Gästequartieren hat man einen herrlichen Blick auf das grüne Flusstal des Ayung. Sayan kann mit drei Spa-Villen aufwarten, die die elegante balinesische Architektur der Anlage widerspiegeln. Natürliche Materialien und traditionelles Design gehen hier eine prachtvolle Verbindung ein. Besondere Beachtung verdienen die handgewebten Seidenstoffe aus Sulawesi, die maßgefertigten Terrazzo-Massagetische sowie die palmblattgedeckten Dächer. Alle Spa-Villen sind auch für Paar-Behandlungen ausgelegt. Die angeschlossenen, halb offenen Badepavillons verfügen über Dampf-, Freiluftduschen und großzügige Badewannen, von denen aus man den Blick auf begrünte Innenhöfe genießt. Zu den aromatischen Anwendungen des Spa gehören das Ingwer-Peeling, der Basilikum-Rosmarin-Bodywrap sowie eine balinesische Massage. Ein Höchstmaß an Entspannung und Luxus bietet die köstliche Lulur-Sayan-Behandlung. Dieses javanische Schönheitsritual beginnt mit einem Kräuterpeeling, auf das ein kühlendes Jogurtbad folgt. Danach wird man mit einem beruhigenden Ylang-Ylang-Blütenbad und einer entspannenden balinesischen Massage mit Bergblütenölen verwöhnt. Nach dieser Verjüngungskur für Körper und Seele wird ein Jamu-Kräuterelixier gereicht, um das Ritual zu vollenden.

WELLNESS-SPECIAL: LULUR SAYAN

À dix minutes d'Ubud, le centre culturel et artistique de l'île, le Four Seasons Bali de Sayan est une retraite exotique, avec 18 suites luxueuses et 42 villas isolées, toutes équipées d'une piscine privée et d'une vue à couper le souffle sur la vallée de l'Ayung. Les trois villas du spa reflètent l'élégance de l'architecture balinaise, dans laquelle les matériaux naturels s'unissent aux formes traditionnelles : meubles recouverts de soie des Célèbes tissée à la main, tables de massage en terrazzo, toitures de chaume. Elles sont adaptés aux soins en couple, et communiquent avec des pavillons de bains extérieurs dotés de douches à vapeur. De grands bassins jouxtant des douches en plein air dominent des jardins privés. Les soins aux épices proposés par le spa comprennent le gommage corporel au gingembre rouge, l'enveloppement au basilic et au romarin, et le massage balinais. Le summum de la relaxation reste le soin du corps Lulur Sayan, rituel de beauté javanais qui débute par un gommage exfoliant aux herbes, se poursuit par une application de yaourt rafraîchissant, puis un bain de pétales d'ylang-ylang, et se termine par un massage balinais aux vertus relaxantes avec une lotion parfumée aux fleurs des montagnes. Le corps et l'esprit ainsi régénérés, la dégustation du jamu, un élixir à base de plantes et d'épices, vient parachever le rituel.

SOIN PHARE : SOIN DU CORPS LULUR SAYAN

Four Seasons Resort Bali at Sayan
Sayan, Ubud, Gianyar 80571
Bali, Indonesia

TEL: +62 361 977577
FAX: +62 361 977588
EMAIL: res.bali@fourseasons.com
WEBSITE: www.fourseasons.com

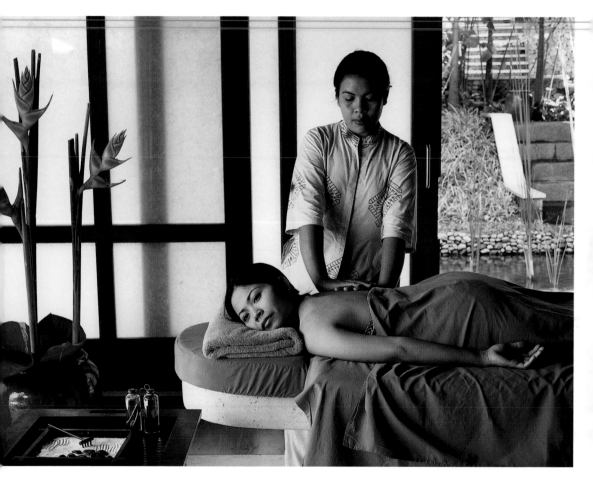

Waroeng Djamoe Spa
at Hotel Tugu Bali

Hotel Tugu Bali was built to re-create and preserve Balinese life, culture, and romance of the past. Set in the Canggu district near an ancient Balinese fishing village, the Hotel Tugu Bali nestles amid lush paddy fields near Batu Bolong Temple, one of Bali's most sacred sites. The resort, which features its own surfing beach, is only a 15-minute drive from the tourist areas of Kuta and Legian. Twenty-two thatched luxury suites and pavilions, constructed in traditional Balinese style, are set beside or over wild lotus ponds – exotic luxury is standard in each. The spa combines spirituality with physical treatment to achieve ultimate relaxation. Waroeng Djamore Spa offers treatments using traditional Balinese methods and all natural ingredients. Unique offerings include the Gemulai Penari Bali, a decadent eight-hour day of treatment, the Pijitan Dandang Watoe (a two-hour hot stone massage), and the Mandi Luhur, inspired by the traditional Javanese wedding ceremony preparation that a woman receives each day during the week preceding the wedding day itself. Other distinctive offerings that help to preserve and perpetuate Indonesia's cultural traditions include Tugu Bali's Gourmet Package, which includes everything from cooking classes to traditional Javanese meals to high tea at sunset.

SIGNATURE TREATMENT: GEMULAI PENARI BALI

Das Hotel Tugu Bali wurde errichtet, um das alte, romantische Bali wieder aufleben zu lassen und seine Kultur zu bewahren. Das in Canggu, unweit eines alten balinesischen Fischerdorfes gelegene Hotel, ist von üppigen Reisfeldern umgeben. Ganz in der Nähe befindet sich der Batu-Bolong-Tempel, eines der berühmtesten Heiligtümer Balis. Von der Anlage, die über einen hauseigenen Surf-strand verfügt, sind es mit dem Auto nur 15 Minuten bis zu den Sehenswürdigkeiten von Kuta und Legian. An wilden Lotusteichen liegen 22 palmblattgedeckte Luxussuiten und Pavillons im balinesischen Stil. Exotischer Luxus gehört hier zum Standard. Das Spa setzt auf Behandlungen, die Körper und Seele verwöhnen und für maximale Entspannung sorgen. Für die hier angebotenen traditio-nell balinesischen Therapien werden nur natürliche Zutaten verwendet. Wellness-Specials sind das Gemulai Penari Bali (eine üppi-ge achtstündige Anwendung), das Pijitan Dandang Watoe (eine zweistündige Massage mit heißen Steinen) sowie das Mandi Luhur. Letzteres orientiert sich an einer javanischen Zeremonie vor Hochzeiten, bei der die Braut in der Woche vor der Eheschließung täg-lich verwöhnt wird. Zu den Angeboten, die die kulturellen Traditionen Indonesiens bewahren und weitergeben wollen, gehört auch das Tugu-Bali-Gourmet-Paket. Darin sind unter anderem ein Kochkurs, traditionell javanische Gerichte sowie eine Teestunde bei Sonnenuntergang enthalten.

WELLNESS-SPECIAL: GEMULAI PENARI BALI

L'Hôtel Tugu de Bali a été créé dans le but de perpétuer le mode de vie, la culture et la douceur de Bali. Situé près de Canggu, un ancien village de pêcheurs, non loin du temple de Batu Bolong – l'un des lieux les plus sacrés de l'île – il est entouré de rizières verdoyantes. Doté de sa propre plage de surf, il n'est qu'à un quart d'heure de route des sites touristiques de Kuta et de Legian. 22 pavillons et suites, de style traditionnel balinais, parmi les bassins de lotus sauvages, font du luxe exotique une règle. Le spa combine spiritualité et trait-ment physique pour atteindre la relaxation maximale. Les méthodes thérapeutiques balinaises traditionelles proposées ici n'em-ploient que des ingrédients naturels. Entre autres soins exclusifs, le spa propose le Gemulai Penari Bali (un traitement de huit heures), le Pijitan Dandang Watoe (deux heures de massages aux pierres chaudes), et le Mandi Luhur (inspiré des sept jours rituels de préparation à la cérémonie de mariage). Incontournable également, l'Assortiment gourmet de Tugu Bali comprend des cours de cui-sine, des repas javanais typiques ainsi qu'un thé traditionnel face au soleil couchant.

SOIN PHARE: GEMULAI PENARI BALI

Waroeng Djamoe Spa at Hotel Tugu Bali
Jl. Pantai Batu Bolong
Canggu Beach
Bali, Indonesia

TEL: +62 361 731701
FAX: +62 361 731708
EMAIL: bali@tuguhotels.com
WEBSITE: www.tuguhotels.com

Losari Coffee Plantation Resort & Spa

Perhaps the perfect destination for a caffeine addict in search of relaxation, the Losari Resort and Spa sits on a working sixty-acre coffee plantation in the Central Java highlands. The spa, designed by Italian architects Andrea and Fabrizio Magnaghi, consists of multiple architectural styles. Each villa has a different feel, from Dutch colonial architecture to Javanese *limasan*. The lobby exudes an eastern ambience with its blue mosaic tiles, white marble floor, and the atmospheric music of the region wafting through the rooms. Losari's spa features six private treatment rooms, with a double unit for couples as well as a *hamam* – a traditional, three-room Turkish steambath. Each section is equipped for both traditional wet and dry treatments. On the lower level, rooms have their own private jacuzzi with a scenic view of the valley. Treatments incorporate Indonesian herbal recipes and traditional beauty treatments from the Royal Javanese Palaces. When they are not being slathered with coffee, guests can learn about the subject on site: Losari owner Gabriella Teggia has devised a series of daily outings through the mountains and villages of the coffee plantation to highlight the traditional techniques still in use today. In this way, the visitor can begin to appreciate the history and significance of coffee on the island of Java.

SIGNATURE TREATMENT: LOSARI EXPERIENCE MASSAGE

Für Koffeinsüchtige mit Erholungsbedarf gibt es kein besseres Reiseziel als das Losari Resort mit Spa, das mitten in einer sechzig Morgen großen Kaffeeplantage im Herzen des Hochlands von Java liegt. Das Spa, das von den italienischen Architekten Andrea und Fabrizio Magnaghi entworfen wurde, verbindet verschiedene Architekturstile. Jede Villa hat eine andere Atmosphäre – vom niederländischen Kolonial- bis hin zum javanischen *Limasan-Stil*. Die Lobby mit ihren blauen Mosaikfliesen und weißen Marmorböden verbreitet ein fernöstliches Flair, während stimmungsvolle Musik aus der Region die Räume durchflutet. Das Losari-Spa umfasst sechs private Behandlungszimmer, eines, das speziell für Paare gedacht ist, sowie einen *Hamam* – das traditionelle, aus drei Räumen bestehende, türkische Dampfbad. Jeder Bereich ist so ausgestattet, dass auch Wasserbehandlungen vorgenommen werden können. Die Räume im Erdgeschoss besitzen alle einen eigenen Jacuzzi, von dem man einen herrlichen Blick auf das Tal hat. Für die Anwendungen werden indonesische Kräuterrezepturen aus den javanischen Königspalästen verwendet. Wenn die Gäste nicht gerade mit Kaffee eingecremt werden, erfahren sie viel über diese Kulturpflanze: Die Eigentümerin des Losari-Resorts, Gabriella Teggia, bietet eine Reihe von Tagesausflügen in die Berge und Dörfer der Kaffeeplantage an, bei denen man einiges über die traditionellen Verfahrensweisen erfährt, die bis heute im Gebrauch sind. Auf diese Weise lernt der Besucher die Geschichte und Bedeutung des Kaffeeanbaus für die Insel Java kennen und schätzen.

WELLNESS-SPECIAL: LOSARI-EXPERIENCE-MASSAGE

Au cœur d'une plantation de café d'une vingtaine d'hectares sur les hauteurs de Java-Centre, le Losari Coffee Plantation Resort and Spa est sans doute l'endroit rêvé pour les accros du café en quête de relaxation. Le spa, conçu par les architectes italiens Andrea et Fabrizio Magnaghi, est un mélange de styles architecturaux. Chaque villa possède un caractère différent, de la demeure coloniale néerlandaise au *limasan* javanais. Le hall d'entrée a des tonalités orientales, avec ses mosaïques bleues, son sol de marbre blanc et la douce musique environnante qui imprègne les lieux. Le spa dispose de six salles de soins privées, dont une pour les couples, ainsi que d'un *hammam* (trois salles de bains turcs traditionnels). Chaque section est équipée pour les soins classiques secs et humides. Au niveau inférieur, chacune des chambres dispose d'un jacuzzi privatif avec vue imprenable sur la vallée. Soins aux herbes d'Indonésie et soins de beauté traditionnels des palais royaux javanais font partie des spécialités de l'établissement. Quand ils ne sont pas enduits de café, les clients peuvent en apprendre un peu plus sur le sujet grâce aux excursions journalières organisées dans l'enceinte de la plantation par la propriétaire de l'établissement, Gabriella Teggia. En découvrant les techniques traditionnelles toujours en usage à l'heure actuelle, les hôtes pourront ainsi apprécier et comprendre l'histoire du café sur l'île de Java.

SOIN PHARE : MASSAGE LOSARI

Losari Coffee Plantation Resort & Spa
Desa Losari · Grabag PO Box 108
Magelang 56100
Central Java, Indonesia

TEL: +62 298 596333
FAX: +62 298 592696
EMAIL: info@losaricoffeeplantation.com
WEBSITE: www.losaricoffeeplantation.com

Inn Seiryuso

Silence, but for the babbling of a mountain stream and the harmony of birdsong. Pavilions artfully arranged among willows and bamboo. A Japanese garden raked and sculpted to serene perfection. Steam rising from still, deep pools. The Inn Seiryuso, a traditional ryokan inn, offers Zen and the art of onsen, the hot spring baths so intrinsic to Japanese culture. Here, as throughout much of the countryside, subterranean springs spout the scalding water that prompted the national passion for bathing and a cleansing ritual as steeped in tradition as the tea ceremony. Wearing yukata, the customary thin cotton gowns, bathers are led to gurgling private tubs carved of green slate, their rounded forms designed for luxuriating. Pails and dippers lie beside the pool for the pre-soak wash, a customary cleansing that precedes a soak in the steaming waters, which reach a stress-dissolving 104°F. Mists drift over the water, obscuring and then revealing the surrounding mountains. Loose-limbed and in a state of floppy euphoria, guests may indulge in shiatsu, reflexology, and other massage techniques in the privacy of their rooms. As evening descends, futons are spread over the straw tatami mats that carpet the 24 guestrooms and 6 suites, a good night's sleep all but guaranteed.

SIGNATURE TREATMENT: ONSEN HOT SPRING BATHS

Sprudelnde Gebirgsquellen und melodisches Vogelgezwitscher, sonst Stille. Kunstvoll um Weiden und Bambus gruppierte Pavillons. Ein perfekt gestalteter japanischer Zen-Garten. Dampf steigt aus stillen, tiefen Becken auf. Neben der Kunst des Zen bietet das Inn Seiryuso, ein traditionelles ryokan-Hotel, noch onsen an, das in der japanischen Kultur so beliebte heiße Bad. Wie überall im Land sprudeln auch hier heiße Quellen, die bei den Japanern zu einer nationalen Badeleidenschaft geführt haben. Ein Reinigungsritual, das aus diesem Land ebenso wenig wegzudenken ist wie seine Teezeremonie. Bekleidet mit einem yukata, einem dünnen Baumwollkimono, schreitet der Gast zu seinem eigenen sprudelnden Natursteinbecken aus grünem Schiefer, dessen runde Formen zum Verweilen einladen. Daneben warten Bottich und Kelle, denn bevor man sich in dem dampfenden, 40°C heißen Wasser aalt, gilt es sich gründlich zu waschen. Nebel steigen auf, verwehen und geben den Blick auf die Berge frei. Entspannt durch das Quellbad, kann man sich anschließend auf dem eigenen Zimmer mit Shiatsu, Reflexzonen- oder anderen Massagen verwöhnen lassen. Abends werden in den mit Tatami-Matten bedeckten 24 Gästezimmern und sechs Suiten die Futons ausgerollt, dann steht einer erholsamen Nacht nichts mehr im Wege.

WELLNESS-SPECIAL: ONSEN (HEISSES QUELLBAD)

Le silence, troublé uniquement par le murmure d'une source et le chant des oiseaux. Des pavillons disposés harmonieusement parmi les saules et les bambous. Un jardin japonais qui touche à la sérénité absolue. La vapeur s'élevant de bassins calmes et profonds. L'Inn Seiryuso, un ryokan – auberge japonaise traditionnelle –, pratique le Zen et l'art de l'onsen, les bains dans les sources d'eau chaude chères à la culture japonaise. Dans le parc du spa, comme dans toute la campagne, jaillissent des sources auxquelles le Japon doit sa passion des bains et des rituels de purification, aussi profondément ancrés dans son histoire que la cérémonie du thé. Vêtus de fins yukatas de coton, les baigneurs sont conduits à des baignoires privées d'ardoise verte, aux formes arrondies et attirantes. Près du bassin, un seau permet de se savonner avant de se plonger dans le bain, dont la température – 40°C – est idéale pour éliminer le stress. L'eau joue avec la brume qui masque et révèle les montagnes environnantes. Dans l'intimité des chambres, une fois parfaitement détendu, euphorique, il est possible de savourer des séances de shiatsu, de réflexologie ou de divers massages. Les futons sont déroulés sur les tatamis, et la nuit s'avance dans les 24 chambres et six suites.

SOIN PHARE: SOURCES CHAUDES ONSEN

Inn Seiryuso
2-2 Kochi
Shimoda 415-0011
Shizuoka, Japan

TEL: +81 558 22 13 61
FAX: +81 558 23 20 66
EMAIL: info@seiryuso.co.jp
WEBSITE: www.seiryuso.co.jp

Ark Hills Spa

Ark Hills Spa was created with but one purpose: for its guests to attain the perfect balance of good health in mind and body. The British firm of Conran & Partners designed a beautiful contemporary environment for this luxurious health and fitness club, situated in the Ark Towers in Tokyo, an ideal base for frequent business travelers to Japan. A reception area clad in cedarwood opens onto the main circulation zone, which is surrounded by a glowing glass wall lit from behind. The cycle of color washes changes constantly, creating different ambiences. The overall effect of the space, an interesting alternative to the more traditional Japanese retreats, is bright, minimal, and slightly futuristic. Ark Hills offers an extensive array of massage treatments including ayurvedic, shiatsu, deep tissue, and sports. Acupuncture is also available on the premises. Ark Hills' Line-up of aesthetic treatments, like the Gift from the Ocean facial mask, is designed to restore vitality to face and body. Their state-of-the-art sauna, jet bath, and Jacuzzi invigorate the senses and lessen body fatigue. Fitness programs, from stretching to aquatics to aerobics, are also offered.

SIGNATURE TREATMENT: AYURVEDIC TREATMENTS

Das Ark Hills Spa hat sich nur eines zum Ziel gesetzt: Die Gesundheit, Fitness und seelische Ausgeglichenheit seiner Gäste. Für den luxuriösen Health- und Fitness-Club in den Ark Towers von Tokyo hat die britische Firma Conran & Partners ein wunderschön zeitgemäßes Design entwickelt – der ideale Rückzugsort für Geschäftsreisende, die häufiger in Japan unterwegs sind. Aus der mit Nadelholz verkleideten Rezeption kommt man in die Halle, die von einer indirekt beleuchteten Glaswand begrenzt wird. Verschiedene Farben tauchen jeden Bereich in eine andere Atmosphäre. Das helle, minimalistische, fast schon futuristisch angehauchte Design ist eine willkommene Abwechslung zu den eher traditionell gehaltenen japanischen Erholungsoasen. Das Ark Hills Spa bietet Ayurveda-, Shiatsu- und Tiefengewebsmassagen an. Verschiedene Sportarten runden das Angebot ab. Sogar Akupunktursitzungen werden hier durchgeführt. Kosmetikbehandlungen wie die Algenmaske sollen Gesicht und Körper neue Vitalität verleihen. Sauna, Whirlpool und Jacuzzi lassen keine Wünsche offen, verwöhnen die Sinne und vertreiben jede Müdigkeit. Diverse Fitnessprogramme (von Stretching über Aquafitness bis hin zu Aerobic) gehören ebenfalls zum Angebot.

WELLNESS-SPECIAL: AYURVEDA-BEHANDLUNGEN

Ark Hills Spa a été créé dans un but précis: permettre à ses hôtes d'atteindre un équilibre parfait du corps et de l'esprit. La société anglaise Conran & Partners a conçu un environnement contemporain pour ce luxueux centre de remise en forme situé dans les Ark Towers de Tokyo, idéal pour les hommes et les femmes d'affaires en voyage au Japon. La réception, toute en bois de cèdre, donne sur le hall central entouré d'un mur de verre éclairé par-derrière, et dont les couleurs changent en permanence, créant ainsi des ambiances très différentes. L'espace est lumineux, minimaliste, presque futuriste – un contraste aux lieux plus traditionnels. Ark Hills offre un vaste choix de massages – ayurvédiques, shiatsu ou massage des tissus profonds – et de sports, ainsi que des séances d'acupuncture. En matière de soins esthétiques, le masque facial «Don de l'océan» est une véritable source de bien-être pour le visage et le corps. Sauna, bain bouillonnant et jacuzzi stimulent les sens et éliminent la fatigue. Des programmes de fitness – stretching, aquagym et aérobic – sont également proposés.

SOIN PHARE: TRAITEMENTS AYURVÉDIQUES

Ark Hills Spa
1-3-40 Roppongi
Minato-ku 106 0032
Tokyo, Japan

TEL: +81 3 55732830
FAX: +81 3 55732835
EMAIL: arkhillsspa@mori.co.jp
WEBSITE: www.hillsspa.com

Roppongi Hills Spa

The Roppongi Hills Spa is set within the new Roppongi complex in Tokyo, Japan, which includes a new Grand Hyatt with 389 rooms and suites, cinema multiplex, art center, business tower, luxury residences, and upscale shops and restaurants. Members of the Roppongi Club enjoy a retreat from the bustle of Tokyo in this sophisticated 1800 square-meter spa designed by Britain's Conran & Partners. Conceived as a journey away from the tension, stress, and fatigue of city living, the spa visitor passes through a series of layers and thresholds, creating in him or her a calm, serene, and enhanced state. To accentuate the notion of the visitor's journey throughout the spa, the design team developed two distinct areas: a "preparatory" side – a cleansing and restrained environment aimed at calming – and a "restorative" side – a more vibrant atmosphere promoting renewed stimulation. The lockers, showers and changing areas on the preparatory side of the plan assist patrons in unwinding, in readiness for the restoration process ahead. The "restorative" side of the spa is meant to enhance purification, stimulation, meditation, and rejuvenation, incorporating whirlpool baths, plunge pools, a swimming pool, and treatment rooms. Vibrantly colored spaces, such as the treatment rooms, provide an atmospheric and stimulating backdrop for the activities within.

SIGNATURE TREATMENT: SHIATSU MASSAGE

Das Roppongi Hills Spa befindet sich im neuen Roppongi-Komplex in Tokyo, zu dem außerdem ein neues Grand Hyatt-Hotel mit 389 Zimmern und Suiten, ein Multiplex-Kino, eine Kunstgalerie, ein Büroturm, Luxus-Apartments sowie exklusive Geschäfte und Restaurants gehören. In dem eleganten, 1.800 Quadratmeter großen Spa, das von den britischen Designern Conran & Partners entworfen wurde, erholen sich die Mitglieder des Roppongi-Hills-Club von der Hektik der Großstadt. Das auf verschiedenen Ebenen angelegte Spa lädt zu einer Reise ein, bei der man den Alltag weit hinter sich lassen kann. Zu diesem Zweck hat das Design-Team zwei strikt voneinander getrennte Bereiche geschaffen: Einen schlicht gestalteten Ruhebereich, der in erster Linie der Entspannung dient, sowie einen belebenden, stimulierenden Anwendungsbereich, der neue Kräfte wecken soll. Die Spinde, Duschen und Umkleideräume im Ruhebereich sind so gestaltet, dass sich der Gast sofort wohl fühlt und auf das vor ihm liegende Programm eingestimmt wird. Der Anwendungsbereich mit seinen Whirlpools, Wasser- und Schwimmbecken soll den Organismus entschlacken, stimulieren und verjüngen. Die lebhaften Farben der Behandlungsräume liefern die atmosphärische Kulisse für die jeweiligen Anwendungen.

WELLNESS-SPECIAL: SHIATSU-MASSAGE

Le Roppongi Hills Spa fait partie du nouveau complexe Roppongi à Tokyo, qui comprend également un hôtel Grand Hyatt avec 389 chambres et suites, un multiplexe, une galerie d'art, une tour de bureaux, des résidences de standing, ainsi que des restaurants et des boutiques de luxe. C'est dans les 1 800 mètres carrés de ce spa sophistiqué conçu par les Britanniques Conran & Partners que les membres du Roppongi Club trouvent refuge contre l'agitation tokyoïte. Tout y est conçu comme une invitation à l'évasion pour se libérer de la tension, du stress et de la fatigue de la vie quotidienne. Après avoir franchi une enfilade de portes et sas, le visiteur se laisse envahir par la sérénité des lieux. Pour renforcer la notion de parcours, deux zones distinctes ont été prévues. La première, pour se préparer: un environnement restreint, pour se ressourcer et se détendre. La seconde, pour se régénérer: une ambiance plus tonique, plus stimulante. Vestiaires et douches, dans la première zone, aident à laisser ses soucis au-dehors et à se préparer pour la suite. La seconde zone favorise purification, stimulation, méditation et régénération, grâce à des bains bouillonnants, des piscines et bassins variés, et des salles de soins. Ces dernières, décorées de couleurs vives, créent une ambiance propice aux activités qui y sont proposées.

SOIN PHARE: MASSAGE SHIATSU

Roppongi Hills Spa

6-12-3 Roppongi
Minato-ku 106-0032
Tokyo, Japan

TEL: +81 3 64066550
FAX: +81 3 64066551
EMAIL: roppongihillsspa@mori.co.jp
WEBSITE: www.hillsspa.com

Pearl Farm Beach Resort

The Pearl Farm Beach Resort is tucked away in a secluded cove of Samal Island in the Philippine Gulf of Davao. The name pays homage to the resort's original incarnation as a pearl farm, where pink, white, and gold oysters from the Sulu Sea were cultivated for their creamy gems. Today, the resort hosts international cognoscenti yearning for natural beauty and unrivaled privacy. Blessed with beaches of white sand, abundant marine life, lush vegetation, and fragrant flora, the island provides a natural sanctuary for its guests. Drawing inspiration from the surrounding terrain, rooms are designed to preserve the cultural history of the island. Samal tribal huts supported by stilts in the water give way to hilltop Balay houses with verandas overlooking the beach and Mandaya houses with sweeping vistas. At the Ylang Ylang Soothing Lounge, guests can enjoy spa treatments outdoors amid gently swaying coconut palms to the music of the ocean. The Asmara Royal Massage – the spa's signature, two-hour treatment – is offered with a menu of essential oils to choose from, including ylang ylang from the flower indigenous to the region. Its exotic and rich aroma is instantly soothing and relaxing.

SIGNATURE TREATMENT: ASMARA ROYAL MASSAGE

Das Pearl Farm Beach Resort liegt ganz versteckt in einer abgeschiedenen Bucht von Samal Island, einer zu den Philippinen gehören-den Insel im Golf von Davao. Sein Name verweist auf die ursprüngliche Nutzung der Anlage als Perlenfarm, wo rosa, weiße und gol-dene Austern aus der Sulusee wegen ihrer cremefarbenen Schätze gezüchtet wurden. Heute genießen die internationalen Spa-Gäste die Schönheit der Natur und die Abgeschiedenheit, die ihnen die Pearl Farm bietet. Die mit weißen Stränden, reicher Meeresfauna, üppiger Vegetation und duftenden Pflanzen verwöhnte Insel ist für ihre Gäste eine einzigartige Ruheoase. Die Gestaltung der Zimmer nimmt die Atmosphäre der Umgebung auf und trägt so zur Bewahrung der kulturellen Identität der Insel bei. Auf Pfählen über dem Wasser schweben die für Samal Island typischen Eingeborenenhütten und machen Häusern im Balay- und Mandaya-Stil Platz, von deren Veranden aus man einen atemberaubenden Meerblick genießt. In der „Ylang Ylang Soothing Lounge" können sich die Gäste inmitten von Palmen, die sich zum Rauschen des Meeres hin und herwiegen, behandeln lassen. Die Asmara Royal Massage – das zweistündige Wellness-Special des Spas – hat eine ganze Palette von essenziellen Ölen im Angebot, darunter auch Ylang Ylang von der gleichnamigen, hier heimischen Blume. Ihr exotischer, überwältigender Duft wirkt auf Anhieb beruhigend und entspan-nend.

WELLNESS-SPECIAL: ASMARA ROYAL MASSAGE

Niché au cœur d'une crique abritée de l'île de Samal dans le golfe de Davao, aux Philippines, le Pearl Farm Beach Resort doit son nom à son ancien statut de ferme perlière. En effet, plusieurs variétés d'huîtres perlières de la mer de Sulu y étaient cultivées pour leurs précieuses perles. Aujourd'hui, l'établissement accueille des connaisseurs du monde entier désireux de se laisser séduire par la beauté naturelle et la douce intimité qu'offre le Pearl Farm. Plages de sable fin, vie marine abondante, végétation luxuriante, flore aux sen-teurs exquises... L'île est un véritable sanctuaire naturel pour ses hôtes. S'inspirant de la nature environnante, la conception des chambres reflète une volonté de préservation de l'histoire culturelle de l'île. Des huttes sur pilotis typiques de Samal côtoient des maisons Balay en hauteur avec vérandas donnant sur la plage et des maisons Mandaya offrant de splendides vues panoramiques. Au Ylang Ylang Soothing Lounge, les soins peuvent également être prodigués en extérieur, à l'ombre des cocotiers se balançant au gré du vent et au rythme de la douce musique de l'océan. Soin phare de l'établissement, le massage royal Asmara, d'une durée de deux heures, est proposé avec de nombreuses variétés d'huiles essentielles, dont l'ylang-ylang, originaire de la région. Son parfum riche et exotique procure une sensation immédiate de bien-être et d'apaisement.

SOIN PHARE: MASSAGE ROYAL ASMARA

Pearl Farm Beach Resort
Kaputian, Island Garden City of Samal
Davao Del Norte
Philippines

TEL: +63 2 7501898
FAX: +63 2 7501894
EMAIL: pearlfarm@fuegohotels.com
WEBSITE: www.fuegohotels.com

The Island Spa
at the Four Seasons Resort Maldives

On a private island in the Indian Ocean, on a coral atoll teeming with brilliant marine life, the Four Seasons Resort Maldives is the ultimate in far-flung luxury. A half-hour trip by speed launch takes guests to the island of Kuda Haraa, where 106 thatched bungalows and villas await on the beach or on stilts over the lagoon. The spa experience is unique: The Island Spa is also set on its own island, accessible by dhoni (the traditional wooden boat of the Maldives). Five thatched-roof treatment pavilions built for couples lie at the beach edge, above the ocean itself. In each pavilion, sliding wooden doors open for fragrant breezes and panoramic views of the sea, while portholes underneath the massage beds allow guests to view the water from their face cradles. Oversized two-person tubs, outdoor garden showers, and aromatic oil burners add an extra element of romance. Treatments run the gamut from ayurvedic traditions from India to traditional body elixirs from Indonesia. The native Maldivian Monsoon Ritual uses ground sandalwood for a scrub, rosewater for a rinse, and frankincense body lotion to moisturize in an indulgent 120-minute experience. Nautical roping, sheer curtains, and design elements from India and Morocco imbue the spa with exotic flavor.

SIGNATURE TREATMENT: MALDIVIAN MONSOON RITUAL

Das auf einem Korallenatoll im Indischen Ozean gelegene Four Seasons Resort bedeutet Luxus pur. Mit dem Schnellboot werden die Gäste in einer halben Stunde auf die Insel Kuda Haraa gebracht, wo 106 palmblattgedeckte Bungalows und Villen auf sie warten. Diese liegen entweder direkt am Strand oder als Pfahlbauten über der Lagune. Das dazugehörige Spa ist ein einzigartiges Erlebnis: Hura Fundhu liegt auf einer eigenen Insel, zu der man mit dem *dhoni*, einem typisch maledivischen Boot, hinübersegelt. Die Anwendungen erfolgen in fünf Pavillons direkt am Strand, die speziell für Paare eingerichtet sind. Die Holzschiebetüren lassen jederzeit eine frische Meeresbrise herein und bieten einen herrlichen Blick auf die Lagune. Gesichtsöffnungen in den Massagebänken gewähren zudem Einblick in die Unterwasserwelt. Großzügige Badewannen für zwei Personen, Gartenduschen und Duftlampen sorgen für eine romantische Atmosphäre. Das Wellness-Angebot umfasst das Beste aus der ayurvedischen Tradition Indiens und reicht bis zu Behandlungen mit indonesischen Heilelixieren. Das Maledivische Monsun-Ritual der Ureinwohner beinhaltet ein Peeling mit Sandelholz, Rosenwasser-Güsse und das Auftragen einer feuchtigkeitsspendenden Weihrauch-Körperlotion – eine zweistündige Verwöhn-Behandlung par Excellence. Fischernetze, transparente Vorhänge und Design-Elemente aus Indien und Marokko verleihen dem Spa seine exotische Atmosphäre.

WELLNESS-SPECIAL: MALEDIVISCHES MONSUN-RITUAL

Situé sur une île privée de l'Océan Indien, au milieu d'un atoll de corail bouillonnant de vie marine, le Four Seasons Resort Maldives représente le luxe absolu. En une demi-heure, la vedette arrive à l'île de Kuda Haraa. Les 106 bungalows et villas aux toits de chaume sont répartis sur la plage ; certains, sur pilotis, sont même dans le lagon. Le spa, sur l'île toute proche de Hura Fundhu, est unique au monde ; on y accède en *dhoni* (bateau traditionnel en bois). Les pieds dans l'eau, cinq pavillons sont conçus pour les soins en couple. Les portes s'ouvrent sur une mer aux brises parfumées, et des ouvertures dans le sol permettent de contempler l'eau tout en recevant les soins. Les immenses baignoires pour deux, les douches dans les jardins et les brûle-parfums rendent l'ambiance plus romantique encore. La palette de soins va des traditions ayurvédiques d'Inde aux secrets des élixirs d'Indonésie. Le Rituel de la mousson des Maldives consiste en un gommage à la poudre de santal, un rinçage à l'eau de rose, et l'application d'une lotion à l'encens – deux heures de plaisir des sens. Les matériaux utilisés pour la décoration – cordages de bateaux, rideaux de fin voilage, objets indiens et marocains – créent une ambiance exotique.

SOIN PHARE : RITUEL DE LA MOUSSON DES MALDIVES

The Island Spa
at the Four Seasons Resort Maldives
Kuda Huraa, North Malé Atoll
Republic of Maldives

TEL: +960 6644 888
FAX: +960 6644 800
EMAIL: world.reservations@fourseasons.com
WEBSITE: www.fourseasons.com

The Lalu

Located in the center of Sun Moon Lake, Taiwan's largest freshwater lake, and entirely surrounded by jade-green mountains, the lush Lalu is a calming place of ancestral worship formerly occupied by the Shao Aboriginal tribe. The Lalu offers stunning accommodations in 95 suites and rooms and a serene setting for a world-class spa experience. The Lalu Spa and Rejuvenation Center focuses on Eastern and Western restorative treatments using only the best natural curatives, including revitalizing Turmeric & Green Tea, Grapefruit & Rose, or Cinnamon & Tangerine body scrubs. Traditional Asian and Western massages are offered as well as breathtaking lake-view steam and sauna facilities. The spa also has hot, warm, and icy whirlpools, herbal steam rooms, dry Swedish saunas, and Japanese bathing facilities overlooking the shimmering lake. When not being pampered at the spa, visitors can make for nearby temples, tribal villages, and stone sculpture gardens. Additional cultural activities can, and should, be arranged. Tea-lovers take note: nearby Mt. Mao Lon is one of the world's largest suppliers of Assam tea. Not to be missed is a visit to Black Tea Factory, built in 1930s Sri Lankan style and dedicated to research in and improvement of tea. It is surrounded by acres of tea plants with picturesque views of Taiwan's mountains.

SIGNATURE TREATMENT: JARI MENARI ("DANCING FINGERS")

Mitten im Sonne-Mond-See, Taiwans größtem Süßwassersee, und umgeben von jadegrünen Bergen liegt Lalu, eine ehemalige Kultstätte des Shao-Stammes. Mit seinen exklusiven Unterbringungsmöglichkeiten in 95 Suiten und Zimmern sowie der wunderbaren Landschaftskulisse ist The Lalu eine erstklassige Wellness-Erfahrung. Das Spa hat sich auf eine Kombination aus östlichen und westlichen Behandlungsmethoden spezialisiert. Für die Peelings aus Gelbwurz & Grünem Tee, Grapefruit & Rose oder Zimt & Mandarine werden nur die besten natürlichen Zutaten ausgewählt. Östliche und westliche Massagetechniken gehören ebenso zum Angebot wie Dampfbad und Sauna, die beide über eine atemberaubende Aussicht verfügen. Außerdem hat das Spa noch heiße, warme und eiskalte Whirlpools, Kräuterdampfräume, eine schwedische Sauna sowie japanische Badeeinrichtungen zu bieten, alle mit Seeblick. Wer sich nicht gerade im Spa verwöhnen lässt, unternimmt Ausflüge zu den nahe gelegenen Tempeln, Dörfern und Skulpturengärten. Darüber hinaus können noch viele weitere kulturelle Unternehmungen gebucht werden. Teeliebhaber aufgepasst: Der nahe gelegene Berg Mao Lon ist eines der größten Anbaugebiete für Assam-Tee. Die Besichtigung der Schwarzteefabrik sollte man sich auf keinen Fall entgehen lassen. Hier dreht sich alles um die Erforschung und Verfeinerung dieses köstlichen Getränks. Das 1930 im Sri-Lanka-Stil errichtete Gebäude liegt inmitten von Teeplantagen und bietet einen herrlichen Blick auf die Berge Taiwans.

WELLNESS-SPECIAL: JARI MENARI („TANZENDE FINGER")

Situé au milieu du lac du Soleil et de la Lune – le plus grand lac d'eau douce de Taïwan – et entouré de montagnes d'un vert de jade, le Lalu est un lieu historique auquel la tribu ancestrale des Shaos a légué une atmosphère toute empreinte de spiritualité et de sérénité. Dans le calme et le confort de l'établissement avec 95 suites et chambres, les traitements revitalisants peuvent agir avec une efficacité maximale. Le centre de remise en forme combine des techniques orientales et occidentales, en n'utilisant que les meilleurs produits naturels comme des gommages revitalisants safran-thé vert, rose-pamplemousse ou cannelle-tangerine. Il propose aussi des massages asiatiques et européens, et dispose d'un sauna et d'un hammam avec une vue inoubliable sur le lac. Après les soins, on peut visiter aux alentours les temples, villages traditionnels et jardins peuplés de sculptures anciennes. D'autres activités culturelles sont également à conseiller. Le mont Mao Lon est l'un des principaux lieux de production du thé d'Assam. On peut visiter la Black Tea Factory, construite dans les années 1930 dans le style du Sri Lanka et destinée à étudier et améliorer le thé, entourée de plantations de thé et qui offre une vue pittoresque sur les montagnes environnantes.

SOIN PHARE: JARI MENARI («LA DANSE DES DOIGTS»)

The Lalu
142 Jungshing Road
Yuchr Shiang Nantao
Taipei, Taiwan 555 R.O.C

TEL: +886 49 285 6888
FAX: +886 49 285 5688
EMAIL: reservations@thelalu.com.tw
WEBSITE: www.thelalu.com.tw

The Oriental Spa

A geographic as well as a spiritual retreat from the bustle of the modern city, The Oriental Spa is a short, picturesque boat ride across the Chao Phya River from The Oriental, Bangkok which offers 358 rooms and 35 suites. The century-old traditional teakwood house, filled with native orchids and redolent of the delicate scent of lemon grass, was restored with indigenous elements – teak floors, Thai antiques, soft filtered light, a long lily pond – that evoke a time when writers like Joseph Conrad, Graham Greene, and Somerset Maugham were regular guests of the hotel. In the spa, the air of meditative calm extends into the luxurious treatment suites (equipped with private steam room and shower) where the loudest sound is the rustle of the therapists' silk uniforms. Many of the treatments draw on ancient Thai techniques and incorporate pure botanicals grown for the spa in the northern hills of Chiang Mai. For example, skin is primed for the signature Oriental Herbal Wrap with an exfoliating scrub made of honey mixed with mint and lavender leaves, flowers, and seeds. Sealed under a thermal wrap, the moisturizing body mask of white Thai mud, camphor, mint, turmeric, and tamarind mingled with sesame oil and fresh milk restores skin while exerting a deliciously rejuvenating effect upon the spirit.

SIGNATURE TREATMENT: ORIENTAL HERBAL WRAP

Dank seiner geografischen Lage ist das Oriental Spa der ideale Rückzugsort, um sich vom hektischen Großstadtleben zu erholen. Vom Oriental Hotel Bangkok mit seinen 358 Zimmern und 35 Suiten trennt es nur eine kurze, malerische Bootsfahrt über den Chao-Phya-Fluss. Das Jahrhunderte alte, orchideengeschmückte und nach Zitronengras duftende Teakholzhaus wurde ausschließlich aus einheimischen Baumaterialien errichtet: Bodendielen aus Teak, thailändische Antiquitäten, gedämpftes Licht und ein lang gestreckter Lilienteich lassen die Zeit wieder aufleben, als hier noch Schriftsteller wie Joseph Conrad, Graham Greene und Somerset Maugham zu Gast waren. Die ruhige, meditative Atmosphäre reicht bis in die luxuriösen Behandlungs-Suiten hinein, die alle über ein eigenes Dampfbad und eine private Sauna verfügen. Das einzige Geräusch, das man hier hört, ist das Rascheln der Masseurskittel. Viele Anwendungen beruhen auf uralten thailändischen Behandlungsmethoden. Gearbeitet wird ausschließlich mit Pflanzen, die in den Hügeln von Chiang Mei extra für das Spa angebaut werden. Beim Wellness-Special, dem fernöstlichen Kräuter-Wrap, erhält man zunächst ein Peeling aus Honig sowie Blättern, Blüten und Samen von Minze und Lavendel. Danach folgt eine warme, feuchtigkeitsspendende Körperpackung aus weißem Thaischlamm, Kampfer, Minze, Gelbwurz und Tamarinde, gemischt mit Sesamöl und frischer Milch. Das verwöhnt nicht nur die Haut, sondern belebt auch den Geist.

WELLNESS-SPECIAL: FERNÖSTLICHER BODYWRAP MIT KRÄUTERN

À l'écart du tumulte et du stress de la ville moderne, l'Oriental Spa et l'Oriental Hotel de Bangkok avec 358 chambres et 35 suites sont chacun sur une rive du Menam Chao Phraya – la traversée, en bateau, est très pittoresque. Le bâtiment en bois de teck, rénové dans le respect des traditions (antiquités thaïes, bassin de fleurs de lis, bois locaux) renferme le souvenir des grands écrivains qui l'ont fréquenté : Joseph Conrad, Graham Greene et Somerset Maugham entre autres. La lumière tamisée et l'atmosphère sereine baignent le spa et les salles de soins, dans lesquels le silence n'est troublé que par le discret bruissement des tenues en soie du personnel. La plupart des soins proposés viennent de techniques thaïes et tirent le meilleur de plantes cultivées sur les collines de Chiang Mai spécialement pour l'établissement. Le soin phare, un enveloppement oriental aux herbes, régénère l'esprit et sublime la peau grâce à un gommage au miel mêlé de menthe et de lavande – feuilles, fleur et graines – suivi d'un masque corporel hydratant composé de boue blanche de Thaïlande, de camphre, de menthe, de safran et de tamarin, mélangés à de l'huile de sésame et à du lait frais, et dont les effets sont décuplés par l'application de serviettes chaudes.

SOIN PHARE : ENVELOPPEMENT ORIENTAL AUX PLANTES

The Oriental Spa
The Oriental, Bangkok
48 Oriental Avenue
Bangkok 10500, Thailand

TEL: +66 2 6599000
FAX: +66 2 6599284
EMAIL: orbkk-reservations@mohg.com
WEBSITE: www.mandarinoriental.com

Chiva-Som
International Health Resort

The exclusive beach resort of Hua Hin is the setting for Chiva-Som ("haven of life"), where holistic spa treatments and medical wellness programs are blended with uniquely Thai hospitality. Styled after a traditional village, the 57 pavilions and suites are surrounded by tropical gardens, waterfalls, and lakes. A staff-to-guest ratio of almost four to one makes for gracious, unhurried service. The modern spa facility comprises more than 40 treatment rooms, surrounded by landscaped courtyards and lounges with rattan chaises and pitchers of lemon-grass-infused water. There are special rooms with flat mats for Thai massage, and six hydrotherapy rooms with French water massage baths and a flotation tank. Fitness options include tai chi and Thai kick boxing in an open pavilion overlooking the sea, and power walks along the beach or to nearby temples. The medical center schedules private health and wellness consultations with each guest upon arrival; along with Western and traditional Chinese medicines, it offers alternative medicine programs such as equilibropathy (which can be used to treat ailments from arthritis to migraines) and iridology (the study of the eyes). An organic garden provides many of the ingredients for the truly mouthwatering spa cuisine, featuring exotic fruits artfully carved in the Thai tradition.

SIGNATURE TREATMENT: TRADITIONAL THAI MASSAGE

Das exklusive Strandhotel von Hua Hin bildet die Kulisse für Chiva-Som, den „Hafen des Lebens". Dort kann man sich nicht nur von ganzheitlichen Spa-Behandlungen und medizinischen Wellness-Programmen, sondern auch von der einzigartigen thailändischen Gastlichkeit verwöhnen lassen. Die wie ein landesübliches Dorf gestalteten 57 Pavillons und Suiten liegen inmitten von tropischen Gärten, Wasserfällen und Seen. Hier kommen auf einen Gast vier Mitarbeiter – da ist ein aufmerksamer Service garantiert. Das moderne Spa verfügt über mehr als 40 Behandlungsräume, die auf romantische Innenhöfe hinausgehen. Lounges mit Rattanliegen, in denen große Krüge mit Zitronengraslimonade bereitstehen, laden zum Verweilen ein. Darüber hinaus gibt es noch mit flachen Matten ausgelegte Räume für die Thai-Massage, sechs Hydrotherapie-Räume mit französischen Wassermassagebecken und einen „Flotation tank". Außerdem kann man Kurse in Tai Chi sowie Thai-Kickboxen belegen, die in einem offenen Pavillon mit Meerblick stattfinden. Power-Walking am Strand oder zu den nahe gelegenen Tempeln steht ebenfalls auf dem Programm. Bei der Ankunft bietet das Medical Center eine individuelle Gesundheits- und Wellness-Beratung an. Neben der westlichen Schul- und der Traditionellen Chinesischen Medizin versteht man sich hier auch auf alternative Heilverfahren. Dazu gehören die Equilibropathie, die bei Arthritis und Migräne hilft, oder die Irisdiagnostik. Im hauseigenen Biogarten wächst Obst und Gemüse, das in der Hotelküche zu köstlichen Gerichten verarbeitet wird. Ein besonderer Augenschmaus sind die exotischen Früchte, die nach Thai-Tradition mit kunstvollen Ornamenten verziert werden.

WELLNESS-SPECIAL: TRADITIONELLE THAI-MASSAGE

Sur la plage de Hua Hin, Chiva-Som (« paradis de vie ») est un spa holistique conçu comme un village traditionnel où les soins de santé et de bien-être se combinent à l'hospitalité thaïe. Jardins tropicaux, chutes d'eau et lacs offrent un écrin de rêve aux 57 suites et villas. Avec quatre employés par curiste, le service est efficace et attentif. Les installations comprennent plus de 40 salles de soins, devant lesquelles on savoure une infusion de mélisse glacée dans des cours et des salons meublés de rotin. Certaines pièces sont équipées de matelas extra-plats pour les massages thaïlandais. Six salles d'hydrothérapie sont dotées de baignoires à jets massants et d'un bain flottant. Les séances de taï-chi et de boxe thaïe ont lieu dans un pavillon ouvert sur la mer, et celles de marche rapide se déroulent sur la plage ou près des temples voisins. Le centre médical offre à l'arrivée au spa des consultations privées de santé et bien-être ; outre des remèdes chinois et occidentaux, il propose des programmes d'équilibropathie (efficace par exemple contre l'arthrite et la migraine) et d'iridologie (examen de l'iris). Le potager biologique fournit la plupart des produits nécessaires à une cuisine délicieuse et saine, parmi lesquels des fruits exotiques artistiquement sculptés selon les traditions locales.

SOIN PHARE : MASSAGE THAÏLANDAIS TRADITIONNEL

Chiva-Som International Health Resort
73/4 Petchkasem Road
Hua Hin, Prachuab Khirikhan 77110
Thailand

TEL: +66 32 536536
FAX: +66 32 511154
EMAIL: reserv@chivasom.com
WEBSITE: www.chivasom.com

Amanpuri

Imagine a luxurious Thai pavilion set on a former coconut plantation endowed with exotic flowers and surrounded by the deep azure Andaman Sea. This vision isn't a dream but an idyllic reality known as Amanpuri on the Thai island of Phuket. Amanpuri means "peaceful place," and the resort with its 40 pavilions and 30 villas lives up to its name. The intimate and secluded grounds offer privacy, while staff members are eager to cater to guests' every need. The spa is a sanctuary: each private spa room features its own changing area, steam shower, treatment area, and outdoor sala (pavilion) for lounging. The spa also has a separate sauna and steam room. Services include a range of massage and holistic therapies, facials, scrubs, body wraps, baths, and beauty treatments, with salas for meditation and yoga sessions. For the signature Aman Spa Special, therapists identify personalized imbalances and assign specialized methods different for each client. Aman takes advantage of ancient Thai beauty secrets such as Look Pra Kob Body Treatment, which uses special local herbs.

SIGNATURE TREATMENT: AMAN SPA SPECIAL, LOOK PRA KOB BODY TREATMENT

Stellen Sie sich einen luxuriösen Thai-Pavillon auf einer ehemaligen Kokosnuss-Plantage vor, der von exotischen Blumen und dem kristallklaren Andamanischen Meer umgeben ist. Dieses Idyll gibt es wirklich, und zwar auf der thailändischen Insel Phuket. Die Anlage mit 40 Pavillons und 30 Villen heißt Amanpuri, „Ort des Friedens", und macht ihrem Namen alle Ehre. Die abgeschiedene Lage garantiert Privatsphäre, während die Mitarbeiter den Gästen jeden Wunsch von den Augen ablesen. Das Spa ist eine Oase der Ruhe. Jeder Spa-Raum verfügt über eine eigene Umkleide, Dampfdusche, Behandlungsbereich sowie eine halboffene *sala* (Pavillon) zum Ausruhen. Außerdem gibt es noch eine separate Sauna sowie ein Dampfbad. Angeboten wird eine Reihe von Massagen und ganzheitlich ausgerichteten Anwendungen. Gesichtsbehandlungen, Peelings, Bodywraps, Bäder und Kosmetik stehen ebenfalls auf dem Programm. In den *Salas* kann man meditieren und Yogaübungen machen. Beim Aman-Spa-Wellness-Special ermitteln die Therapeuten zunächst die Problemzonen und stellen dann ein individuelles Behandlungsprogramm zusammen. Dabei greifen sie auf uralte Schönheitsgeheimnisse Thailands zurück wie die Look-Pra-Kob-Ganzkörperbehandlung, bei der diverse einheimische Kräuter zum Einsatz kommen.

WELLNESS-SPECIAL: AMAN-SPA-SPECIAL, LOOK-PRA-KOB-GANZKÖRPERBEHANDLUNG

Un luxueux pavillon thaï, à l'emplacement d'une ancienne plantation de cocotiers, entre des massifs de fleurs exotiques et le bleu profond de la mer d'Andaman... Ce paradis existe sur l'île thaïlandaise de Phuket : il s'agit de l'Amanpuri, « lieu de paix », qui mérite largement son nom. L'établissement avec 40 pavillons et 30 villas, intime et protégé, s'attache à satisfaire toutes les envies de ses clients. Le spa est un véritable sanctuaire : chaque zone privée dispose de ses propres vestiaires, bain de vapeur, salle de soins et *sala* (pavillon) extérieur. En plus d'un sauna et d'un hammam, les services proposés comprennent massages et thérapies holistiques, masques, gommages, enveloppements, bains et soins esthétiques, ainsi que des séances de méditation et de yoga dans les *salas*. Le Spécial Spa Aman permet au praticien d'identifier les déséquilibres internes et de mettre au point des méthodes individualisées pour rétablir l'harmonie. Le soin du corps Look Pra Kob, à base de plantes traditionnelles, est un concentré des secrets de beauté des thaïlandaises d'autrefois.

SOIN PHARE: SPECIAL SPA AMAN, SOIN DU CORPS LOOK PRA KOB

Amanpuri
Pansea Beach
Phuket 83000
Thailand

TEL: +66 76 324333
FAX: +66 76 324100
EMAIL: amanpuri@amanresorts.com
WEBSITE: www.amanresorts.com

Caribbean

Shambhala at Parrot Cay

Robert De Niro, Donna Karan, and Demi Moore are among the celebrity guests who have frequented the exclusive Parrot Cay, set on a private 1000-acre island in the Turks & Caicos chain (just an hour-and-a-half flight from Miami). The 60 rooms, beach houses, and villas are almost dazzlingly pale, with bleached-pine floors, whitewashed walls, and four-poster beds swathed in white voile. Weathered terracotta tile roofs, white-railed verandas and white slip-covered couches add to the aesthetic appeal. The Asian-inspired Shambhala spa is a holistic retreat housed in four structures overlooking the island's marshy wetlands. The main building has three massage rooms, each with its own Japanese bath and porch, as well as a sundeck that leads to a 540-square-foot infinity pool; three private pavilions for couples are also available. Traditional Asian therapies – including a 90-minute Thai massage performed by a former Buddhist monk – are offered along with new ayurvedic treatments such as Ahbyanga (a four-handed massage) and Ubtan (a herbal power scrub). Products range from the popular Dr. Hauschka to Invigorate, a skin-care line developed exclusively for Shambhala. Complementary yoga and Pilates classes are offered daily, and special weeklong retreats are regularly scheduled, with visits from international health specialists and yoga instructors.

SIGNATURE TREATMENT: AHBYANGA

Robert De Niro, Donna Karan und Demi Moore gehören zu den prominenten Gästen des Parrot Cay. Die exklusive Anlage befindet sich auf einem 400 Hektar großen Eiland der Turks- und Caicos-Inseln und ist gerade einmal eineinhalb Flugstunden von Miami entfernt. Die 60 Zimmer, Strandhäuser und Villen sind außen und innen weiß gestrichen, besitzen helle Holzfußböden und in weißen Voile gehüllte Himmelbetten. Mit verwitterten Terrakottaziegeln gedeckte Dächer, weiß gestrichene Veranden und weiß bezogene Sofas setzen die puristische Ästhetik fort. Das fernöstlich inspirierte Shambhala-Spa ist ganzheitlich orientiert und besteht aus vier Gebäuden, die alle auf das Sumpfland der Insel hinausgehen. Im Hauptgebäude befinden sich drei Massageräume, die jeweils über ein japanisches Bad, eine Veranda und ein Sonnendeck verfügen. Letzteres geht auf einen 50 Quadratmeter großen Naturpool hinaus. Für Paare stehen drei Privat-Pavillons zur Verfügung. Neben traditionellen asiatischen Behandlungsmethoden wie der 90-minütigen Thai-Massage, die von einem buddhistischen Mönch ausgeführt wird, werden auch neue Ayurveda-Anwendungen wie Ahbyanga (eine vierhändige Massage) oder Ubtan (ein Kräuter-Peeling) angeboten. Die verwendeten Produkte reichen von Dr. Hauschka bis hin zu Invigorate, einer speziell für das Shambala-Spa entwickelten Pflegeserie. Tägliche Yoga- und Pilates-Kurse ergänzen das Programm. Zusätzlich gibt es Wellness-Wochen, für die international bekannte Gesundheitsspezialisten und Yoga-Lehrer anreisen.

WELLNESS-SPECIAL: AHBYANGA

Entre autres célébrités, Robert De Niro, Donna Karan, et Demi Moore ont fréquenté le très select Parrot Cay, situé sur une île privé de près de 400 hectares de l'archipel Turks et Caicos (à une heure et demie d'avion de Miami). Les 60 chambres, bungalows et villas sont clairs, immaculés, avec leur sol en pin, leurs murs chaulés et leurs lits à baldaquins aux voilages blancs. Tuiles de terre cuite, balustrades blanches et sofas ivoire apportent une touche de sérénité à la beauté ambiante. Le Shambhala, d'inspiration asiatique, est un spa holistique composé de quatre édifices dominant les marais. Le bâtiment principal comporte trois salles de massage dotées chacune d'une installation de bains japonais avec patio et d'un solarium donnant sur une piscine à débordement de 50 mètres carrés. Trois pavillons privés, destinés aux couples, sont également disponibles. Des soins traditionnels d'Asie – dont un massage thaïlandais de 90 minutes pratiqué par un ancien moine bouddhiste – sont proposés aux côtés de traitements ayurvédiques de pointe, comme l'Ahbyanga (un massage à quatre mains) et l'Ubtan (un gommage aux plantes), grâce aux produits du Dr Hauschka et à la gamme Invigorate (soins de la peau développés en exclusivité pour Shambala). Des cours de yoga et de Pilates sont dispensés gracieusement, et des semaines de retraite sont organisées régulièrement par des professeurs de yoga et des spécialistes de la santé et du bien-être.

SOIN PHARE: AHBYANGA

Shambhala at Parrot Cay
P.O. Box 164, Providenciales
Turks & Caicos Islands
British West Indies

TEL: +1 649 9467788
FAX: +1 649 9467789
EMAIL: res@parrotcay.como.bz
WEBSITE: www.parrotcay.como.bz

La Samanna

La Samanna, which consists of 81 suites on 55 acres on Baie Longue, a crescent-shaped white-sand beach, evokes a traditional French spirit with a Caribbean soul. Guests come here for a plethora of reasons, among them La Samanna's extensive wine cellar, its gourmet cuisine, breathtaking beach views, and luxe spa treatments. The Elysée Spa boasts indoor/outdoor tropical garden treatment rooms, Pilates studios, and no small number of decadent pampering treatments. The most sought after of these is the Thalatherm, designed by the famous Institut Phytomer in France. After a day of beautifying activities, guests can get some exercise at La Samanna's fitness pavilion, professional tennis courts, or its pool. Each of the Caribbean resort's suites is fully stocked with L'Occitane bath products, loofahs, and aroma candles, allowing guests to continue their own personal spa treatments in the privacy of their own rooms. Also adding to La Samanna's theme of luxury converging with nature are the calming tones in its decor. The interior design is meant to give one the feeling of vacationing in a friend's Mediterranean villa – a very generous friend, that is.

SIGNATURE TREATMENT: THE THALATHERM

La Samanna verfügt über 81 Suiten, die sich auf einem Areal von 25 Hektar auf dem sichelförmigen, weißen Sandstrand von Baie Longue verteilen. Hier treffen französisches Savoir-vivre und karibische Lebensfreude aufeinander. Die Gäste kommen aus vielen Gründen nach La Samanna – nicht zuletzt wegen des sehr gut sortierten Weinkellers, der Feinschmeckerküche, des atemberaubenden Strandes und der erstklassigen Spa-Anwendungen. Das Elysée-Spa bietet geschlossene und halboffene Behandlungsräume, die sich zu einem tropischen Garten öffnen, Pilates-Studios sowie eine Vielzahl von Wellness-Behandlungen. Die beliebteste ist die vom berühmten Institut Phytomer in Frankreich entwickelte Thalatherm, bei der man mit Algenpackungen verwöhnt wird. Nachdem man tagsüber etwas für seine Schönheit getan hat, kann man Abends an einem der Kurse im Fitness-Pavillon teilnehmen, Tennis spielen oder ein paar Bahnen im Pool schwimmen. Damit sich die Gäste in ihren Privaträumen weiter pflegen können, ist jede Suite mit Körperpflegeprodukten von L'Occitane, Luffaschwämmen und Duftkerzen ausgestattet. Zum Konzept von La Samanna, Luxus und Natur miteinander zu verbinden, passt auch das unaufdringliche Ambiente. Hier kommt man sich vor wie in der Mittelmeervilla eines Freundes – eines äußerst großzügigen Freundes, natürlich.

WELLNESS-SPECIAL: THALATHERM

La Samanna, avec ses 81 suites réparties sur les 25 hectares de Baie Longue, une plage de sable blanc en forme de croissant, mêle l'âme des Caraïbes à l'esprit français. On s'y rend pour bon nombre de raisons son impressionnante cave à vin, sa cuisine gastronomique, ses plages d'une beauté à couper le souffle et son spa luxueux. Le spa Élysée propose des salles de soins grandes ouvertes sur un jardin tropical, des salles de Pilates, et presque trop d'occasions de se faire dorloter – la plus tentante étant peut-être le Thalatherm, conçu en France par le célèbre Institut Phytomer. Après une journée de soins esthétiques, la salle de fitness de La Samanna permet de pratiquer par exemple le tennis ou la natation. Toutes les suites sont garnies de produits pour le bain signés L'Occitane, de loofas et de bougies parfumées, permettant ainsi de prolonger les soins dans l'intimité. La décoration rend l'atmosphère de l'établissement plus luxueuse encore, plus paisible, plus agréable. Elle est pensée pour donner l'impression d'être en villégiature dans la villa méditerranéenne d'un ami – un ami particulièrement généreux.

SOIN PHARE: LE THALATHERM

La Samanna
P.O. Box 4077
97064 St. Martin CEDEX
French West Indies

TEL: +590 590 876400
FAX: +590 590 878786
EMAIL: reservations@lasamanna.com
WEBSITE: www.lasamanna.com

Europe

Les Sources de Caudalie

Les Sources de Caudalie (49 rooms and suites) puts a new spin on the French fondness for the grape. While the restaurant features the sort of stellar wine list that is to be expected in the region, treatments concentrate on the lesser-known star qualities of Bordeaux's harvest. Set within the confines of one of the country's most prestigious vineyards, the spa's exterior recalls local vintners' chais, the wooden aging sheds where fine wines are left to develop their flavor. Inside, the yeasty perfume of the grape by-products used in treatments permeates the air. The anti-aging properties of the local Cabernet Sauvignon variety give Caudalie its raisin-d'être. Polyphenols found in the fruit are said to not only reduce the free radicals responsible for aging skin, but also to improve blood circulation. Add the mineral-rich water that springs from underground and a Grand Cru cure is born: Vinothérapie. Treatments can include a "mulling" in a wine barrel-cum-hot tub overlooking fields of prized vines, a vigorous exfoliation using grape-seed powder followed by a grape-seed oil massage, or a detoxifying wine-and-honey wrap that leaves the skin silky smooth. With the body thoroughly renewed from the fruits of the vine, the timbered tisanerie provides a salubrious setting for sipping herbal tea spiked with the vintner's wares.

SIGNATURE TREATMENT: VINOTHÉRAPIE

Im Les Sources de Caudalie mit seinen 49 Zimmern und Suiten wird die französische Vorliebe für Wein neu interpretiert: Während das Restaurant über eine für die Region typische, erstklassige Weinkarte verfügt, setzen die Spa-Anwendungen auf verborgenere Qualitäten des Bordeauxs. Das in einem der berühmtesten Weinanbaugebiete Frankreichs gelegene Spa erinnert auf den ersten Blick an den *chai* eines Weinbauern, eines der verwitterten hölzernen Weinlager, in denen man den Wein reifen lässt. In seinem Innern dagegen duftet es nach den auf Traubenbasis hergestellten Schönheitsprodukten. Die Anti-Aging-Qualitäten des hiesigen Cabernet Sauvignon haben Les Sources de Caudalie berühmt gemacht. Die in den Trauben enthaltenen Polyphenole bekämpfen nicht nur Freie Radikale, die für die Hautalterung verantwortlich gemacht werden, sondern regen auch die Durchblutung an. Jetzt muss man sich nur noch die mineralhaltigen, unterirdischen Quellen dazudenken, und die „Grand-Cru-Kur" namens Vinotherapie ist perfekt. Zur Behandlung gehört ein heißes Bad in einem Weinfass, von dem aus man den Blick über prämierte Weinberge genießen kann. Dann folgen ein gründliches Peeling auf Traubenkernbasis, wahlweise eine Massage mit Traubenkernöl oder eine Entschlackungspackung aus Wein und Honig, die für eine samtweiche Haut sorgen. Dementsprechend verjüngt, setzt man sich in die Fachwerk-*tisanerie*, wo es sich herrlich an mir Wein verfeinerten Kräutertees nippen lässt.

WELLNESS-SPECIAL: VINOTHERAPIE

Les Sources de Caudalie avec 49 chambres et suites renouvellent l'amour de la France pour la vigne et le vin. Au restaurant, la carte de vins est sublime, et les soins proposés par le spa mettent à profit des qualités moins connues des crus locaux. Situé dans l'un des vignobles les plus prestigieux du Bordelais, le spa rappelle les chais, ces abris dans lesquels on donne le temps aux grands crus de développer leur saveur. À l'intérieur, le parfum des sous-produits de la vigne utilisés pour les soins imprègnent l'air. Les propriétés anti-âge du cabernet sauvignon sont la « raisin d'être » du spa. Les polyphénols du raisin combattent les radicaux libres responsables du vieillissement de la peau et améliorent la circulation sanguine. Associés à une eau riche en minéraux, ils font de la vinothérapie le Grand Cru des cures. Parmi les soins proposés, le Bain barrique avec vue sur les vignes, un gommage énergique avec de la poudre de pépins de raisins suivi d'un massage à l'huile de pépins de raisins, ou un enveloppement au miel et au vin, détoxifiant, qui laisse la peau d'une douceur de soie. Une fois le corps régénéré grâce à la vigne, la tisanerie permet de déguster des infusions relevées à la mode locale.

SOIN PHARE : VINOTHÉRAPIE

Les Sources de Caudalie
Chemin de Smith Haut Lafitte
33650 Bordeaux-Martillac
France

TEL: +33 5 57838383
FAX: +33 5 57838384
EMAIL: sources@sources-caudalie.com
WEBSITE: www.sources-caudalie.com

Brenner's Park-Hotel & Spa

A landmark 19th-century hotel in a private park overlooking the River Oos, Brenner's Park-Hotel & Spa was originally built to house the cosmopolitan elite that flocked to Baden-Baden to take the waters. (As far back as Roman times, Baden-Baden was known throughout Europe for the curative powers of its thermal springs.) Brenner's Spa is a modern take on old-world rejuvenation, with areas titled Relaxarium (retreat) and Frigidarium (an open-air cold plunge pool), along with a Japanese garden, traditional Finnish sauna, and individual aroma whirlpools. The private spa suite comes with its own whirlpool, sauna, and shower, along with a Japanese Flower Blossom Steam Bath, scented with jasmine and orchid blossom, and a Laconicum, with warm benches of green quartzite. Signature treatments include the Maharaja Massage Mystics – in which a therapist uses only legs and feet to massage the body and hands only on the head and scalp – and Inner Illumination, in which Bulgari beauty products are used in a uniquely indulgent fashion. The Black Forest Clinic, also on the Brenner's complex, specializes in internal medicine; the fitness center has an aerobics studio and a terrace for outdoor exercise. Guests of the 100-room hotel also exercise in the hotel pool, surrounded by frescoes and Ionic columns.

SIGNATURE TREATMENT: ORIENTAL BODY MASK, MASSAGE RITUALS, MAHARAJA MASSAGE MYSTICS

Das in einem privaten Park über der Oos gelegene Brenner's Park-Hotel & Spa ist ein Juwel aus dem 19. Jahrhundert. Gebaut wurde es für die internationale Hautevolée, die damals nach Baden-Baden zur Kur kam. (Für die Heilwirkung seiner Thermalquellen war Baden-Baden allerdings schon zur Römerzeit in ganz Europa bekannt.) Brenner's Spa ist die moderne Variante dieses historischen Jungbrunnens. Es verfügt über Relaxarium (Ruheraum), Frigidarium (Kalttauchbecken im Freiluftbereich), einen japanischen Garten, Finnische Sauna sowie diverse Whirlpools mit Aromazusätzen. Darüber hinaus gibt es noch eine private Spa-Suite. Dazu gehören Whirlpool, Sauna, Dusche, ein nach Jasmin und Orchideen duftendes japanisches Blütendampfbad sowie ein Laconicum mit beheizten Bänken aus grünem Quarzit. Eines der Wellness-Specials nennt sich „Maharaja Massage Mystics". Dabei massiert der Therapeut ausschließlich mit Beinen und Füßen, nur am Kopf wird mit den Händen gearbeitet. Außerdem im Angebot: das Beauty-Programm „Inner Illumination", bei dem der Gast ausgiebig mit Kosmetikprodukten von Bulgari verwöhnt wird. Die Schwarzwaldklinik, die sich ebenfalls auf dem Hotelgelände befindet, ist auf Innere Medizin spezialisiert. Ferner gibt es noch ein Fitness-Center mit Aerobic-Studio und Terrasse zum Training im Freien. Selbstverständlich können sich die Gäste des 100-Zimmer-Hotels auch im hoteleigenen Hallenschwimmbad tummeln, das mit Fresken und ionischen Säulen geschmückt ist.

WELLNESS-SPECIAL: MAHARAJA MASSAGE MYSTICS

Ce prestigieux hôtel du XIXᵉ siècle, avec son parc privé qui domine l'Oos, a été construit afin d'accueillir l'élite cosmopolite qui se pressait à Baden-Baden pour prendre les eaux. Sous l'empire romain déjà, la ville était renommée pour la vertu curative de ses sources. Le spa de Brenner est une interprétation moderne d'une tradition ancestrale. Le relaxarium est un lieu de repos, le frigidarium une piscine extérieure aux eaux fraîches. Jardins japonais, sauna finlandais traditionnel, bains à remous individuels : tout est fait pour le bien-être. Le spa privé dispose de son propre bain à remous, d'un sauna, de douches, d'un bain de vapeur aux fleurs – venu du Japon – aux senteurs de jasmin et d'orchidée, d'un laconicum où se reposer sur des bancs chauffés de quartzite vert. L'un des soins phares, le Massage mystique Maharaja, est un massage lors duquel on utilise les jambes et les pieds pour masser le corps, et les mains pour la tête. L'autre, la Lumière intérieure, met à profit les qualités de produits bulgares pour une beauté toute en douceur. La clinique de la Forêt-Noire, qui dépend du complexe, est spécialisée en médecine interne. Le centre de fitness dispose d'un studio d'aérobic et d'une terrasse pour les activités en plein air. Les clients de l'hôtel avec 100 chambres peuvent profiter d'une piscine entourée de fresques et de colonnes ioniques.

SOIN PHARE: MASSAGE MYSTIQUE MAHARAJA

Brenner's Park-Hotel & Spa
Schillerstraße 4–6
76530 Baden-Baden
Germany

TEL: +49 7221 9000
FAX: +49 7221 387732
EMAIL: information@brenners.com
WEBSITE: www.brenners.com

Blue Lagoon

Its dramatic, otherworldly setting – steam rising from intensely blue water backed by mountains and gleaming architecture – makes the Blue Lagoon the most photographed site in Iceland. An hour's drive from Reykjavik, the "lagoon" is actually the runoff from a nearby power plant that forms a pool of geothermal water, with temperatures that range between 100 and 110°F. The pool is rich in beneficial natural minerals (salts, silica, and blue algae), which give the lagoon its color. People started bathing in the lagoon in 1981, and patients with skin conditions such as psoriasis began touting the waters' curative powers. At the spa, water is completely refreshed every 24 hours; you can rent a bathing suit, robe, and towel and simply soak, wandering through waterfalls, hot spots, sauna, steam bath, and lava caves. In-water massages and body treatments, from spa facial to salt glow, are available, as well as holistic treatments. Facilities are open year-round, ideal for enjoying summer's long days or the preternatural calm of winter. There's also a sleek, Scandinavian-modern restaurant overlooking the waters, serving seafood from a nearby fishing village. The entire Blue Lagoon experience is as cool and bizarre as Iceland itself.

SIGNATURE TREATMENT: SILICA MASSAGE

Seine einzigartige Lage macht das Blue Lagoon zur meist fotografierten Sehenswürdigkeit Islands. Mit dem dampfenden, blauen Wasser, den Bergen und der funkelnden Architektur wirkt es wie aus einer anderen Welt. Die etwa eine Stunde von Reykjavik entfernte „Lagune" ist ein geothermischer Pool mit zwischen 38 °C und 43 °C heißem Wasser, der zu einem nahe gelegenen Kraftwerk gehört. Der Pool enthält eine Vielzahl von natürlichen Mineralien (Salze, Kieselerde, Blaualgen), die der Lagune ihre intensive Farbe verleihen. Gebadet wird hier seit 1981. Seitdem rühmen vor allem Patienten mit Psoriasis und anderen Hautkrankheiten die Heilwirkungen dieses Wassers, das alle 24 Stunden komplett ausgetauscht wird. Badeanzug, Bademantel und Handtuch können gemietet werden. Anschließend aalt man sich im warmen Wasser, durchquert Wasserfälle oder besucht Sauna, Dampfbad und Lava-Höhle des Spa. Hier werden Unterwasser-Massagen, Körper- und Gesichtsbehandlungen und ein Salzpeeling sowie ganzheitliche Anwendungen angeboten. Die Anlage ist das ganze Jahr geöffnet – und somit ideal geeignet, um dort einen langen Sommer- oder einem kalten Wintertag zu verbringen. Mit dabei: Ein modernes Restaurant im skandinavischen Stil mit Meerblick, das Meeresfrüchte aus dem nahe gelegenen Fischerdorf serviert. Die Blaue Lagune ist so cool und bizarr wie Island selbst.

WELLNESS-SPECIAL: KIESELERDE-MASSAGE

Le paysage, extraordinaire et stupéfiant – la vapeur s'élevant du bleu profond d'une mer entourée de montagnes et de bâtiments lumineux – fait du Blue Lagoon le site le plus photographié d'Islande. À une heure de route de Reykjavik, le « lagon » est en fait le lac de retenue d'un barrage, formant un bassin dont la température varie entre 38° C et 43° C. L'eau est riche en minéraux bienfaisants (sels, silice) et en algues bleues qui lui donnent sa couleur caractéristique. On a commencé à s'y baigner en 1981, et les gens qui souffraient de maladies de peau comme le psoriasis chantaient les louanges de ses vertus curatives. Au spa, l'eau est entièrement renouvelée toutes les 24 heures ; on peut louer maillots, peignoirs, serviettes et savon, se promener au milieu des cascades, profiter du sauna, du hammam et des grottes volcaniques, savourer des massages aquatiques, des soins du corps – du masque jusqu'au soin-éclat au sel – et des traitements holistiques. Le spa est ouvert toute l'année, rendant accessibles les longues journées d'été ou le calme surnaturel de l'hiver. Dominant les eaux, un restaurant moderne sert de la cuisine scandinave et les fruits de mer du village voisin. Le Blue Lagoon est aussi agréable et aussi étrange que l'Islande elle-même.

SOIN PHARE: MASSAGE À LA SILICE

Blue Lagoon
Svartsengi
240 Grindavik
Iceland

TEL: +354 420 8800
FAX: +354 420 8801
EMAIL: bluelagoon@bluelagoon.com
WEBSITE: www.bluelagoon.is

Capri Palace Hotel & Spa

Sitting atop the picturesque Italian island from which it takes its name, the Capri Palace Hotel & Spa offers a home-away-from-home for the peripatetic in search of relaxation and rejuvenation. Modeled on classical Mediterranean lines, the hotel with 77 rooms and suites resembles a gracious palazzo with Romanesque columns, vaulted ceilings, gilt-framed mirrors, and a whiter-shade-of-pale color scheme. In the spa, aptly named the Capri Beauty Farm, the focus is on personal aesthetics. Looking good is taken seriously here, and physicians supervise many of the treatments. Obeying doctor's orders might involve a dip in the hydrotherapy pool followed by a seaweed wrap or a personalized diet and fitness regime drawn up by a team of nutritionists and personal trainers. The signature Leg School focuses on the lower limbs – problems from poor circulation, to cellulite, to varicose veins are diagnosed and then cared for with a course of complementary therapies that combine both traditional and alternative approaches. For example, mud baths and medicated bandages stimulate blood flow while hands-on lymphatic drainage and deep-tissue massage eliminate toxins. School "graduates" report reduced swelling and smoother, sleeker-looking thighs, which have plenty of opportunity for exposure along the popular, sun-drenched lido deck.

SIGNATURE TREATMENT: THE LEG SCHOOL

Das hoch oben auf der italienischen Insel gelegene Capri Palace Hotel & Spa ist für Reisende ein wahres Refugium: Hier kann man sich herrlich entspannen und verjüngen lassen. Das im klassisch-mediterranen Stil gehaltene Hotel mit 77 Zimmern und Suiten wirkt mit seinen prächtigen Säulen, Gewölben, pastellfarbenen Wänden und vergoldeten Spiegeln wie ein eleganter Palazzo. Im Spa mit dem passenden Namen Capri Beauty Farm dreht sich alles um die Schönheit. Hier wird gutes Aussehen wirklich ernst genommen: Viele der Anwendungen werden von Ärzten überwacht. Ein Bad im Hydrotherapie-Pool, gefolgt von Algenpackungen – so könnte das Programm lauten. Auf Wunsch stellt das Team aus Ernährungsberatern und Personal Trainern auch eine individuelle Diät nebst Fitnessprogramm zusammen. Beim Wellness-Special „Leg School" stehen die Beine im Mittelpunkt. Etwaige Probleme wie Durchblutungsstörungen, Zellulitis oder Krampfadern werden diagnostiziert und dann mit mehreren, einander ergänzenden Therapien angegangen. Dabei greift man sowohl auf traditionelle als auch auf alternative Behandlungsformen zurück: Schlammbäder und medizinische Bandagen regen die Durchblutung an, während Lymphdrainagen und Tiefengewebsmassagen beim Entschlacken helfen. Absolventen der „Leg School" berichten von abklingenden Schwellungen und geschmeidigeren Schenkeln ... die sie auf der sonnigen Strandterrasse nur zu gern präsentieren!

WELLNESS-SPECIAL: DIE LEG SCHOOL

Sur les hauteurs de l'île italienne dont il tire son nom, le Capri Palace est un havre de paix pour les voyageurs en quête de relaxation et de régénération. Inspiré de l'architecture méditerranéenne classique, l'hôtel avec ses 77 chambres et suites évoque un *palazzo*, avec ses colonnes romanes, son plafond voûté, ses miroirs anciens et ses murs immaculés. Le spa, la «Capri beauty farm», prend au sérieux la beauté du corps. Beaucoup de soins sont supervisés par des médecins, qui peuvent prescrire un bain dans la piscine d'hydrothérapie suivi d'un enveloppement aux algues, ou, suivant les conseils de nutritionnistes et d'entraîneurs, mettre au point un régime personnalisé et un programme d'exercice physique. Le soin phare met les jambes à l'honneur; problèmes circulatoires, cellulite ou varices sont traités de façon complémentaires par des approches traditionnelles et alternatives. Bains de boues et bandages médicaux stimulent la circulation, drainages lymphatiques manuels et massages profonds éliminent les toxines. Les résultats: décongestionnées, les cuisses sont lissées, affinées, et peuvent s'afficher sur le deck ensoleillé.

SOIN PHARE: SOIN DES JAMBES

Capri Palace Hotel & Spa
Via Capodimonte 2b
80071 Anacapri
Capri, Italy

TEL: +39 0 81 9780111
FAX: +39 0 81 8373191
EMAIL: info@capripalace.com
WEBSITE: www.capripalace.com

Vigilius Mountain Resort

At the very remote and oh-so-stylish Vigilius Mountain Resort (named after St. Vigilius, known for his altruism and intelligence), you can only arrive by cable car or on foot. Though the town is a convenient driving distance from such major cities as Zurich and Milan, the Resort's location atop the South Tyrol's Vigiljoch Mountain ensures that the loudest thing visitors are likely to hear during their stay is the distant sound of cowbells. Matteo Thun, Vigilius's architect, has said that the design of the resort represents for him an investigation between the physical space and the definition of the mental place of nature. Accordingly, the idyllic, Dolomite-framed retreat offers a program that aims far beyond the average, hour-long massage (though this is certainly available). During fall and winter, Vigilius guests have the opportunity to engage in Focus Week, a unique, intensive program designed as "time out" for the improvement of personal health and wellbeing. Guests are encouraged to commit to this Life Modeling Week – specifically designed to influence their life back in the "real world" – twice a year. This thoughtful, integrative approach is similarly expressed in the architecture of Vigilius: the mountain-top resort is not only aesthetically stunning, but environmentally friendly as well.

SIGNATURE TREATMENT: FOCUS WEEKS

Zu dem abgeschiedenen und äußerst stilvollen Vigilius Mountain Resort, dessen Namensgeber Sankt Vigilius berühmt war für seine Bildung und Bescheidenheit, gelangt man nur mit der Seilbahn oder zu Fuß. Obwohl es nur wenige Autostunden von Zürich oder Mailand entfernt ist, sorgt seine Lage hoch oben auf dem Südtiroler Vigiljoch dafür, dass sich die Gäste während ihres Aufenthalts höchstens durch das Läuten von Kuhglocken gestört fühlen können. Für Matteo Thun, den Architekten des Vigilius Mountain Resort, stellt seine Architektur eine Erkundung des physischen Raums und der Definition des inneren Stellenwerts der Natur dar. Dementsprechend wartet die idyllische, von den Dolomiten gesäumte Ruheoase mit einem Programm auf, das weit mehr zu bieten hat als die übliche einstündige Massage (die natürlich auch mit zum Angebot gehört): In der Herbst- und Wintersaison können die Gäste eine so genannte „Focus-Woche" buchen, ein einzigartiges Intensivprogramm, das als Auszeit gedacht ist, in der man sich ganz der Gesundheit und dem persönlichen Wohlbefinden widmet. Idealerweise meldet man sich zweimal im Jahr für diese Selbstfindungs-Woche an, die sich auch auf den normalen Alltag in der „wirklichen Welt" auswirken soll. Dieser intelligente, ganzheitliche Ansatz spiegelt sich auch in der Architektur der Vigilius-Anlage wider: Das hoch in den Bergen gelegene Resort überzeugt nicht nur vom ästhetischen, sondern auch vom ökologischen Standpunkt her.

WELLNESS-SPECIAL: FOCUS-WOCHEN

Lieu de retraite d'une sublime élégance, le Vigilius Mountain Resort (du nom de saint Vigile, célèbre pour son altruisme et son intelligence) n'est accessible qu'à pied ou en téléphérique. Les grandes villes comme Zurich ou Milan sont à une distance raisonnable en voiture. Toutefois, étant donné la position géographique du site, au sommet du Monte San Vigilio dans le Tyrol du Sud, seul le bruit des cloches de vaches parviendra aux oreilles des visiteurs. D'après Matteo Thun, l'architecte du Vigilius Mountain Resort, la conception de cet établissement représente une recherche entre l'espace physique et la définition de la place mentale de la nature. Ainsi, le spa, situé dans le cadre idyllique des Dolomites, propose bien plus que de simples massages d'une heure (sans doute également disponibles). En automne et en hiver, les hôtes du Vigilius Mountain Resort peuvent prendre part à une semaine de recentrage sur soi, programme unique et intensif conçu comme un « temps mort » consacré à l'amélioration de la santé et du bien-être personnel. Deux fois par an, les participants sont invités à adopter un autre modèle de vie le temps d'une semaine, modèle qu'ils pourront essayer de reproduire par la suite dans la « vraie vie ». Cette approche méditative et intégrative se reflète dans l'architecture même du Vigilius Mountain Resort : l'établissement n'est pas simplement d'une esthétique remarquable, il s'intègre parfaitement dans la nature environnante.

SOIN PHARE : SEMAINES DE RECENTRAGE SUR SOI

Vigilius Mountain Resort
Vigiljoch
39011 Lana, Italy

TEL: +39 0473 556600
FAX: +39 0473 556699
EMAIL: info@vigilius.it
WEBSITE: www.vigilius.it

Bulgari Hotel

Italian luxury house Bulgari promises its signature sophistication with a healthy dose of *la dolce vita* at its premier hotel and spa, located in Milan's fashion district. Housed in a former nunnery bordered by botanical gardens, the Bulgari spa is Asian-inspired in its design and features opulent local materials like Vicenza stone and Turkish Afyon marble. The indoor, gold-mosaic pool reflects the ancient tradition of wellness-through-water while also adding the requisite quota of Italian glamor. The spa offers three signature treatments that utilize exclusive Bulgari products, including the all-encompassing Holistic Back, Face, and Scalp Treatment with hot-stone therapy. A detoxifying and intensive facial treatment is the precursor to a relaxing back and scalp massage that uses acupressure to target and relieve stress points. Following this, hot stones are placed along the spine, shoulders, and neck to stimulate vital energy points. A head massage completes the experience. Guests can round off their day in the spa's Turkish baths, its meditation garden, or with a glass of *vino rosso* on the terrace overlooking the property's lush gardens. Bulgari Spa ensures proper pampering for the *fashionista* after a hectic day of shopping on the famous Via Montenapoleone and Via delle Spiga, located just around the corner.
SIGNATURE TREATMENT: HOLISTIC BACK, FACE, AND SCALP TREATMENT

Mit seinem mitten in Mailands In-Viertel gelegenen First Class Spa-Hotel macht der italienische Luxuskonzern Bulgari seinem Namen alle Ehre und verspricht eine gesunde Dosis *dolce vita*. Das Spa, das in einem ehemaligen, von botanischen Gärten gesäumten Nonnenkloster untergebracht ist, verströmt ein asiatisches Flair und prunkt mit kostbaren Baumaterialien wie Vicenza- und Afyon-Marmor. Der mit Goldmosaiken verzierte Innenpool spiegelt die antike Tradition von der wohltuenden Wirkung des Wassers wider und verleiht dem Ganzen einen Hauch italienischen Glamour. Das Spa bietet drei Wellness-Specials an, für die ausschließlich Bulgari-Produkte verwendet werden. Dazu gehört auch die ganzheitliche Rücken-, Gesichts- und Kopfhautbehandlung, bei der mit heißen Steinen gearbeitet wird. Eine entschlackende, intensive Gesichtsbehandlung bereitet auf die entspannende Rücken- und Kopfhautmassage vor, bei der bestimmte Akupressurpunkte stimuliert werden. Anschließend werden entlang der Wirbelsäule sowie auf Schultern und Hals heiße Steine aufgelegt, um Energiepunkte anzuregen. Eine Kopfmassage beendet die Anwendung. Zum Abschluss können die Gäste die zum Spa gehörenden türkischen Dampfbäder, den Meditationsgarten oder die Terrasse aufsuchen, um dort mit einem Glas *vino rosso* den herrlichen Blick auf die üppigen Gärten des Anwesens zu genießen. Das Bulgari Spa bietet das ideale Verwöhnprogramm für *fashionista*, die einen hektischen Einkaufstag auf der berühmten Via Montenapoleone und der Via delle Spiga hinter sich haben. Beide Einkaufsstraßen liegen gleich um die Ecke.
WELLNESS-SPECIAL: GANZHEITLICHE RÜCKEN-, GESICHTS- UND KOPFHAUT-BEHANDLUNG

Située au cœur des quartiers chic de Milan, la luxueuse maison italienne Bulgari abrite un hôtel et un spa de première catégorie, alliant élégance et raffinement qui ne sont pas sans rappeler la *dolce vita*. Ancien couvent entouré de jardins botaniques, le spa Bulgari, d'inspiration asiatique, tire parti de matériaux nobles de la région comme la pierre de Vicence et le marbre d'Afyon. La piscine intérieure, toute de mosaïque dorée, rappelle l'ancienne tradition du bien-être par l'eau tout en ajoutant l'indispensable note de glamour à l'italienne. Le spa propose trois soins à base de produits exclusifs Bulgari, dont le soin holistique du dos, du visage et du cuir chevelu prodigué à l'aide de pierres chaudes. Un masque intensif et détoxifiant précède un massage relaxant du dos et du cuir chevelu. Ce massage fait appel à la digitopuncture pour éliminer les points de tension. Des pierres chaudes sont ensuite appliquées le long de la colonne vertébrale, sur les épaules et sur la nuque afin de stimuler les principaux points d'énergie. Un massage crânien vient compléter le soin. Pour finir la journée, rien de tel qu'un moment de détente aux bains turcs, dans le jardin de méditation ou sur la terrasse donnant sur les jardins luxuriants de l'établissement, en dégustant un verre de *vino rosso*. Au spa Bulgari, les *fashionista* sont l'objet de toutes les attentions après des journées trépidantes passées à faire du shopping sur les célèbres Via Montenapoleone et Via delle Spiga, à deux pas de l'établissement.
SOIN PHARE: SOIN HOLISTIQUE DU DOS, DU VISAGE ET DU CUIR CHEVELU

Bulgari Hotel
Via Privata Fratelli Gabba 7/b
20121 Milan
Italy

. TEL: +39 02 8058051
FAX: +39 02 805805222
EMAIL: milano@bulgarihotels.com
WEBSITE: www.bulgarihotel.com

Grotta Giusti Terme & Hotel

The bucolic Tuscan setting that is home to the Grotta Giusti spa belies the inferno that rages below. Beneath this verdant expanse, the elements have carved out a subterranean cavern where bubbling, mineral-rich waters spew health-enhancing steam. Amid stalactites and stalagmites sculpted through the millennia, guests clad in white cotton tunics lounge on wooden recliners as they sweat out toxins and inhale curative vapors in one of three Dante-esque chambers. Temperatures climb as the levels descend. In Paradise, the thermometer registers 87.8°F. In Purgatory, it hits 89°F. And in Inferno, the lowest chamber, temperatures soar to 93°F, with humidity reaching a sopping 100%. The small but energetic Lake Limbo at the grotto's base is the source of all the thermodynamic action. Back above ground, the stone-clad spa offers a wide range of treatments. Some, like thermal aerosol inhalation, are geared to specific maladies. Others, like hydromassage and a selection of mudpacks, are purely for pleasure. Exercise options are similarly diverse, including everything from yoga to tai chi to aerobics. Nearby, the converted 19th-century villa that houses the hotel with 64 rooms and suites offers a sweat-free zone. Its air-conditioned, antique-filled environs can best be described as an Italianate paradiso.

SIGNATURE TREATMENT: THERMAL STEAM BATH

Die idyllische Landschaft der Toskana, in die sich das Grotta Giusti Spa schmiegt, wirkt wie die Antithese zum tobenden Inferno unter der Erde: Dort hat die Natur unter den grünen Hügeln eine unterirdische Höhle geschaffen, in der wild brodelnde, mineralhaltige Quellen gesunde Dämpfe ausspucken. Inmitten von Jahrtausende alten Stalaktiten und Stalagmiten schwitzen die in weiße Tuniken gehüllten Gäste hier ihre Giftstoffe aus. Das Ganze spielt sich in drei Räumen ab, die nach Dantes „Göttlicher Komödie" benannt sind. Je tiefer man in die Erde vordringt, desto wärmer wird es. Im Paradies zeigt das Thermometer 31°C an, im Purgatorium 32°C. Im am tiefsten gelegenen Inferno klettern die Temperaturen bis auf 34°C bei einer Luftfeuchtigkeit von 100%. Der kleine, aber aktive Limbo-See auf dem Grund der Grotte ist der Urheber dieser thermodynamischen Konstellation. Über der Erde wartet das ganz mit Naturstein verkleidete Spa, das eine Vielzahl von Behandlungen anbietet. Einige, wie die thermale Aerosol-Inhalation, wirken gegen ganz bestimmte Beschwerden. Andere, wie die Hydromassage oder diverse Schlammpackungen, tun einfach nur gut. Auch das Fitness-Angebot ist überaus breit gefächert und reicht von Yoga über Tai Chi bis hin zu Aerobic. Endgültig Schluss mit dem Schwitzen ist im nahe gelegenen Hotel mit 64 Zimmern und Suiten, das in einer ehemaligen Villa aus dem 19. Jahrhundert untergebracht ist. In seinen klimatisierten, mit antikem Mobiliar eingerichteten Räumen fühlt man sich wirklich wie im Paradies.

WELLNESS-SPECIAL: THERMAL-DAMPFBAD

Le paysage typiquement toscan qui entoure le spa Grotta Giusti est l'antithèse absolue de l'enfer du sous-sol: sous la verdure, la nature a creusé une grotte dans laquelle une eau pétillante riche en minéraux se transforme en vapeur aux vertus bénéfiques. Parmi les stalactites et les stalagmites sculptées par le temps dans trois salles dignes de Dante, on se prélasse sur des chaises longues, vêtus de tuniques de cotons, tout en éliminant les toxines et en respirant les vapeurs curatives. Plus on descend, plus la température monte. Au paradis, il fait 31°C. Au purgatoire, 32°C. Et en enfer, la salle la plus basse, près de 34°C – avec 100% d'humidité. Les Limbes, le petit lac de la grotte, est l'origine de la thermodynamique des lieux. À la surface, le spa propose une large gamme de traitements. Certains, comme les inhalations thermales, sont destinés à des affections particulières. D'autres, comme les hydromassages et les enveloppements, ont le plaisir pour seul objectif. La même diversité est de mise dans les programmes de fitness – yoga, taï-chi, aérobic, et bien d'autres disciplines, sont représentées. Non loin, la villa dix-neuvième devenue hôtel avec 64 chambres et suites constitue un délicieux refuge. Air conditionné et meubles d'époque: le paradis est italien.

SOIN PHARE: BAIN THERMAL

Grotta Giusti Terme & Hotel
Via Grotta Giusti 1411
51015 Monsummano Terme
Italy

TEL: +39 05 72 90771
FAX: +39 05 72 9077200
EMAIL: info@grottagiustispa.com
WEBSITE: www.grottagiustispa.com

Les Thermes Marins de Monte-Carlo

Monte-Carlo – the name alone conjures up images of glamour and opulence. The Thermes Marins de Monte-Carlo spa, built at the behest of Prince Rainier III and under the direction of a leading expert in thalasso therapy, fulfills that vision and then some. Pretty in pale pink, the facade's dominating feature is towering arched windows that catch reflections of the Mediterranean shimmering in the nearly year-round sun. An open-air, seafront terrace offers delicious but healthful meals for spa-goers and solace for soleil worshippers. Inside the four-level complex, sunlight likewise bathes the indoor recreational pool, a swimming hole à la Botticelli where saltwater pumped in from the far-off depths of the Mediterranean glistens beneath a seashell-shaped ceiling. A second pool for treatments features built-in jet streams and an assortment of pulsating contrivances. Trained "marine therapists" put these devices to work, relaxing tense muscles and washing away stress as they oversee an array of seawater-based therapies. Apart from the pools, a separate dry zone offers massage rooms with views of the azure sea, a state-of-the-art fitness facility for toning, and a marble-lined hammam for sweating out impurities within a regal milieu.

SIGNATURE TREATMENT: SEAWATER THERAPY

Monte-Carlo – ein Name, der Glamour und Luxus verspricht. Das Spa der Thermes Marins de Monte-Carlo, das auf Geheiß von Fürst Rainier III. erbaut wurde und von einem führenden Experten für Thalasso-Therapie geleitet wird, löst dieses Versprechen ein. Charakteristisch für seine blassrosafarbene Fassade sind die riesigen Bogenfenster. In ihnen spiegelt sich das Mittelmeer, über dem beinahe das ganze Jahr die Sonne scheint. Auf der bei Sonnenanbetern äußerst beliebten Terrasse mit Meerblick bekommen die Spa-Gäste ebenso köstliche wie gesunde Mahlzeiten serviert. Auch das Hallenbad im Innern des vierstöckigen Gebäudes ist sonnendurchflutet. In den Pool à la Botticelli, über den sich eine muschelförmige Decke wölbt, wird Salzwasser aus den Tiefen des Mittelmeers gepumpt. Ein zweiter Pool für Anwendungen verfügt über Jet-Düsen und weitere Massagevorrichtungen. Diese nutzen ausgebildete „Marine-Therapeuten" für eine Vielzahl von Behandlungen auf Meerwasserbasis, die gegen verhärtete Muskeln helfen und für Entspannung sorgen. Neben diesem Pool gibt es Massageräume mit Blick auf das türkisblaue Meer, ein hochmodernes Fitness-Studio sowie einen marmorgefliesten Hamam – ein wirklich fürstliches Ambiente zum Entschlacken!

WELLNESS-SPECIAL: MEERWASSER-THERAPIE

Monte-Carlo – ce nom suffit à évoquer le glamour et le luxe. Le spa des Thermes Marins de Monte-Carlo, construit sous l'impulsion du prince Rainier III et grâce aux conseils des plus grands experts, tient son rang. Sur la façade rose pâle, les hautes fenêtres en ogive reflètent la Méditerranée ensoleillée. Sur la terrasse en front de mer, on peut déguster des repas délicieux et sains, ou se faire bronzer. À l'intérieur, le soleil continue de régner sur les quatre étages : piscine, bassin droit issu d'un tableau de Botticelli où l'eau de mer, pompée dans les profondeurs, miroite sous un plafond en forme de coquillage. Une autre piscine, réservée aux soins, dispose de jets directionnels. Des « thérapeutes marins » formés spécialement les utilisent pour détendre les muscles contractés et éliminer le stress grâce à différentes techniques de thalassothérapie. À l'écart, dans la zone sèche, les salles de massages donnent sur la mer, les salles de fitness sont ultra-modernes, et le hammam de marbre permet d'éliminer les impuretés dans un décor de conte de fées.

SOIN PHARE: THÉRAPIE À L'EAU DE MER

Les Thermes Marins de Monte-Carlo

2, avenue de Monte-Carlo

98000 Monte Carlo

Monaco

TEL: +377 98062525

FAX: +377 98062626

EMAIL: resort@sbm.mc

WEBSITE: www.montecarlospa.com

Sturebadet

Amid the bustle of downtown Stockholm, the Sturebadet's eclectic blend of architectural styles is mirrored in its multicultural approach to well-being. First erected in 1885 under the direction of a Dr. Curman, it was then faithfully restored after a fire a century later – a bust of the founder guards the entrance to the present-day spa. The doctor's visit to a Venetian Renaissance palazzo, the Vendramin-Calergi, inspired the facade. Inside, Moorish arches meld with Italianate colonnades and Nordic gingerbread in a surprisingly harmonious fusion. One floor is dedicated to a Turkish-style bathhouse. Options here include basking in a Finnish sauna, simmering in a marble-lined steam room, or chilling out in the plunge pool where earthy Tuscan colors warm up the ambience. A visit to one or the other might be the perfect finish to the spa's half-day "kur." Based on traditional European cures, this indulgence combines exercise with spa treatments: unlimited use of the high-tech gym's fitness equipment, an exfoliating body scrub, a dunk in the relaxation pool aglow under frosted skylights. And of course an authentic Swedish massage – 25 minutes of Stockholm's indigenous form of bodywork, a thorough, tension-busting kneading and stroking.

SIGNATURE TREATMENT: THE KUR, TURKISH BATH RITUAL

Mitten in der geschäftigen Stockholmer Altstadt steht das Sturebadet, dessen eklektizistische Architektur wunderbar mit seinem multikulturellen Wellnessprogramm harmoniert. Das 1885 unter der Leitung des Medizinprofessors Dr. Curman errichtete Gebäude wurde hundert Jahre später nach einem Brand originalgetreu wieder aufgebaut, wobei die Büste des Gründers heute den Eingang zum Day-Spa ziert. Bei einem Besuch in Venedig ließ sich der Doktor für die Fassade von dem venezianischen Renaissance-Palazzo Vendramin-Calergi inspirieren. Im Innern des Gebäudes gehen maurische Bögen, italienische Kolonnaden und skandinavisches Schnitzwerk im neugotischen Stil eine erstaunlich harmonische Verbindung ein. Ein Stockwerk bildet das türkische Badehaus. Es stehen außerdem eine finnische Sauna, ein marmorgefliestes Dampfbad und ein Tauchbecken zum Abkühlen zur Verfügung. Toskanische Ockertöne sorgen optisch für Wärme. Der Besuch eines dieser Wellness-Bereiche bildet den idealen Abschluss der im Sturebadet angebotenen Halbtagskur. Wie viele traditionelle europäische Kuren verbindet auch sie Sport mit Spa-Anwendungen: Erst trainiert man im hauseigenen Fitness-Studio an den neuesten Hightech-Geräten, anschließend folgen ein Ganzkörper-Peeling und ein kurzes Bad im Entspannungspool, den Oberlichter aus Milchglas angenehm beleuchten. Schlussendlich darf eine echt schwedische Massage nicht fehlen, bei der man nach bester Stockholmer Manier 25 Minuten lang durchgeknetet wird.

WELLNESS-SPECIAL: DIE KUR

Dans l'animation du centre-ville de Stockholm, le Sturebadet, éclectique, multiculturel, mêle plusieurs styles architecturaux et plusieurs approches du bien-être. Construit en 1885 sous l'impulsion du Dr Curman, il a été restauré un siècle plus tard après un incendie. Aujourd'hui un buste du fondateur en orne l'entrée. C'est un palais Renaissance de Venise, le Vendramin-Calergi, qui a inspiré la façade du bâtiment. À l'intérieur, arches maures, colonnades italiennes et éléments d'une richesse toute nordique se fondent en une harmonie inattendue. Un étage entier est occupé par les bains turcs. Se prélasser dans le sauna finlandais, se détendre dans le hammam de marbre ou se rafraîchir dans la piscine aux couleurs chaudes inspirées de la Toscane : trois excellentes façons de parachever la demi-journée de « kur » proposée par le spa. Inspirées des cures européennes traditionnelles, ce moment privilégié comporte à la fois des programmes physiques et des soins de beauté : en plus d'un accès illimité aux équipements de fitness sophistiqués, un gommage corporel, une séance de relaxation dans une piscine éclairée par les lucarnes couvertes de givre et, bien sûr, un authentique massage suédois : 25 minutes de manipulations douces ou plus toniques qui détendent en profondeur.

SOIN PHARE : KUR

Sturebadet
Sturegallerian 36
114 46 Stockholm
Sweden

TEL: +46 8 54501500
FAX: +46 8 54501510
EMAIL: info@sturebadet.se
WEBSITE: www.sturebadet.se

Victoria-Jungfrau Grand Hotel & Spa

Nestled between the picturesque Thun and Brienz lakes at the foot of the Alps in Interlaken, Switzerland, the Victoria-Jungfrau Grand Hotel welcomes visitors seeking the restorative effects of old-world hospitality in an idyllic setting. Offering a full complement of beauty, health, sports, and fitness activities at ESPA, its luxury spa, the Victoria-Jungfrau provides guests with an array of treatments, rituals, and healing services. Inspired by ancient life-giving rituals, ESPA has developed treatments fusing ancient eastern practices and traditions with the latest medical innovations of the west. Indian, Balinese, and Asian rituals and historical practices are among the treatment concepts that merge global techniques and healing philosophies from around the world. ESPA's Signature Ritual, a multi-cultural body treatment, begins with ceremonial foot cleansing. A skin-softening salt and oil scrub for the body comes next, followed by a hydrating facial. The comprehensive ritual continues with a Shiatsu-inspired, free-flowing massage and concludes with an Indian head massage focusing on vital energy points on the scalp and neck. For the guest who also seeks cultural stimulation, the Victoria-Jungfrau offers a wide range of creative pursuits, from T'ai Chi to mountain climbing, music festivals to cookery classes.

SIGNATURE TREATMENT: VICTORIA-JUNGFRAU SIGNATURE RITUAL

Das malerisch am Fuß der Alpen zwischen dem Thuner und dem Brienzer-See gelegene Victoria-Jungfrau Grand Hotel in Interlaken zieht jene Gäste an, die sich nach der wohltuenden Wirkung europäischer Gastlichkeit in einem idyllischen Ambiente sehnen. Das hauseigene Luxus-Spa ESPA mit seinem allumfassenden Schönheits-, Gesundheits-, Sport- und Fitnessprogramm bietet seinen Gästen eine riesige Auswahl an Anwendungen, Ritualen und Wellness-Behandlungen. Angeregt durch uralte, energiespendende Rituale hat man im ESPA Anwendungen entwickelt, die traditionelle fernöstliche Heilpraktiken mit den neuesten medizinischen Erkenntnissen des Westens verbinden. Indische, balinesische und asiatische Rituale sowie traditionelle Anwendungen gehören zu dem Behandlungskonzept, das auf der ganzen Welt bewährte Techniken und Wellness-Philosophien miteinander kombiniert. Das hauseigene Spa-Special, eine multikulturelle Ganzkörperbehandlung, beginnt mit einem zeremoniellen Fußbad. Darauf folgen ein die Haut weich machendes Salz-/Öl-Peeling für den ganzen Körper sowie eine Feuchtigkeitsmaske fürs Gesicht. Das Ritual enthält außerdem eine Art Shiatsu-Massage, die mit einer indischen Kopfmassage abgeschlossen wird. Letztere widmet sich wichtigen Energiepunkten auf der Kopfhaut und im Nacken. Dem kulturinteressierten Gast bietet das Victoria-Jungfrau Grand Hotel ein reichhaltiges Programm, das von Tai-Chi-Stunden über Wanderungen und Musikfestivals bis hin zu Kochkursen reicht.

WELLNESS-SPECIAL: VICTORIA-JUNGFRAU-SPEZIAL-RITUAL

À Interlaken en Suisse, entre les magnifiques lacs de Thoune et de Brienz, le Victoria-Jungfrau Grand Hotel & Spa accueille les visiteurs en quête des bienfaits régénérateurs de l'hospitalité d'antan dans un cadre idyllique au pied des Alpes. Grâce aux activités beauté, santé, sport et fitness dispensées au spa de luxe ESPA, le Victoria-Jungfrau propose une gamme complète de soins, de rituels et de services pour le bien-être de ses hôtes. S'inspirant de rituels ancestraux, l'ESPA a élaboré des soins alliant anciennes pratiques et traditions orientales et dernières innovations médicales du monde occidental. Pratiques et rituels indiens, balinais et asiatiques, s'appuyant sur des techniques et des philosophies de bien-être du monde entier, font partie des soins prodigués au spa. Le rituel Victoria-Jungfrau, soin phare de l'ESPA, est un soin du corps aux origines multiculturelles. Il commence par une purification rituelle des pieds, suivie d'un gommage corporel à base d'huile et de sel, et d'un masque hydratant. Le rituel se poursuit par un massage d'inspiration shiatsu et se termine par un massage crânien à l'indienne centré sur les principaux points d'énergie du cuir chevelu et de la nuque. Pour les visiteurs également désireux d'enrichir leur culture personnelle, le Victoria-Jungfrau propose un large éventail d'activités, du taï chi à l'escalade, en passant par les festivals de musique et les cours de cuisine.

SOIN PHARE: RITUEL VICTORIA-JUNGFRAU

Victoria-Jungfrau Grand Hotel & Spa
Höheweg 14
3800 Interlaken
Switzerland

TEL: +41 33 8282828
FAX: +41 33 8282880
EMAIL: interlaken@victoria-jungfrau.ch
WEBSITE: www.victoria-jungfrau.ch

Lenkerhof Alpine Resort

Neither traditional nor modern, the Lenkerhof Alpine Resort brings a fresh outlook to a grand hotel. Located in the one of the most beautiful valleys in the Swiss Alps, the Lenkerhof is home to the 7sources beauty & spa, named after the seven sources of the local River Simme. The wonderful amenities at this elegant sanctuary are sure to promote relaxation, beauty, health, and fitness. In the grand European spa tradition, special emphasis is placed on the restorative effects of saunas. Indeed, the spa offers not one but seven different ways for guests to work up a sweat. A Finnish version blasts hot, dry air, while the bio sauna delivers cooler air with colored lights, and herb and stone oil saunas put a spin on the traditional sauna experience. Sulfur and ice grottos provide a respite from all that heat. If saunas are not your thing, however, opt instead to enjoy a full-body micro massage while listening to music and sipping champagne in the Crystal Tub. Employing the latest technologies in everything from sound through magnetic field therapies, the Crystal Tub elevates the experience of a simple soak to a completely different level.

SIGNATURE TREATMENT: CRYSTAL TUB

Der Lenkerhof Alpine Resort ist weder traditionell noch modern – er ist ein Grandhotel im neuen Look. Er liegt in einem der schönsten Täler der Schweiz und beherbergt das „7sources beauty & spa", benannt nach den sieben Quellen der Simme. Der elegante Schönheitstempel mit seinen vielen Annehmlichkeiten sorgt mit Sicherheit für die nötige Entspannung, Schönheit, Gesundheit und Fitness. Gemäß der langen europäischen Spa-Tradition legt man besonders großen Wert auf das Saunieren. Und so hält das Spa für seine Gäste nicht nur eine, sondern gleich sieben Möglichkeiten parat, richtig ins Schwitzen zu kommen. Die finnische Version empfängt den Gast mit heißer, trockener Luft, die Biosauna mit gemäßigteren Temperaturen bringt farbiges Licht ins Spiel, während die Kräuter- und Stein-Öl-Saunen die traditionelle Schwitzbaderfahrung auf ein neues Niveau heben. Schwefel- und Eisgrotte sorgen anschließend für eine angenehme Abkühlung. Wer Saunas nichts abgewinnen kann, sollte es stattdessen mit einer Ganzkörper-Mikromassage versuchen, bei der man im „Crystal Bad" mit Musik und Champagner verwöhnt wird. Ausgestattet mit der neuesten Technik, von der Musikanlage bis hin zur Magnetfeldtherapie, macht diese Wanne ein einfaches Bad zu einem unvergesslichen Erlebnis.

WELLNESS-SPECIAL: CRYSTAL BAD

Ni traditionnel, ni contemporain, le Lenkerhof Alpine Resort donne une nouvelle image des grands hôtels. Situé au cœur de l'une des plus belles vallées des Alpes suisses, le Lenkerhof abrite le 7sources beauty & spa, qui doit son nom aux sept sources de la rivière Simme qui coule à proximité. Les équipements de ce luxueux établissement sont entièrement dédiés à la relaxation, à la beauté, à la santé et au fitness. Dans la grande tradition des spas européens, les saunas et leurs effets régénérateurs sont mis à l'honneur. En effet, le 7sources beauty & spa ne propose pas moins de sept façons différentes de prendre un bain de vapeur. Le sauna finlandais souffle un air chaud et sec, tandis que le sauna bio distille un air plus frais aux herbes et aux lumières colorées. Les saunas aromatiques sont, quant à eux, plus traditionnels. La grotte de glace et la grotte d'eau sulfureuse procurent ensuite un agréable moment de fraîcheur. Toutefois, si vous n'êtes pas un inconditionnel du sauna, optez pour le bain Crystal et son micromassage corporel au son d'une douce musique et un verre de champagne à la main. Tirant parti des dernières innovations thérapeutiques (musique et champs magnétiques), le bain Crystal confère une toute nouvelle dimension au bain.

SOIN PHARE: BAIN CRYSTAL

Lenkerhof Alpine Resort
Postfach 241
3775 Lenk im Simmental
Switzerland

TEL: +41 33 7363636
FAX: +41 33 7363637
EMAIL: welcome@lenkerhof.ch
WEBSITE: www.lenkerhof.ch

Therme Vals

Therme Vals appears to be the antithesis of Alpine architectural clichés, yet the monumental edifice belongs thoroughly to the local landscape. Architect Peter Zumthor custom-fitted layer upon layer of locally quarried quartzite slabs (60,000 in all) to create a museum-like venue for the mineral-rich waters that spring from underground. Bathers enter through a subterranean tunnel as though delving into the heart of the mountain. From there, changing rooms let onto a balcony overlooking the main-floor baths – six pools that scale the temperature range from arctic to equatorial. The ice pool hits the mercury at a bone-chilling 57°F, the fire pool at a stress-melting 107°F. Among the options that fall in between is the flower pool, a floral soup packed with fragrant petals and constantly maintained at a comfortable 91°F. Beneath the watery, rock-faced milieu of the baths, rooms painted in metallic silver are the setting for a menu of cures that includes beauty treatments, aromatherapy, thalassotherapy, and massage. Particularly appropriate to the quartzite environs is the spa's signature treatment – a stone massage. For nearly two hours, a therapist slides heated pebbles dipped in aromatic oil over the body, ironing out tension with every stroke. The proprietors promise that Therme Vals' original 140-room hotel will soon be "on a par with the distinction of the Therme Vals."

SIGNATURE TREATMENT: STONE MASSAGE

Die Therme Vals ist das absolute Gegenteil traditioneller Alpenarchitektur. Und trotzdem fügt sich der massive Bau perfekt in seine Umgebung ein. Der Architekt Peter Zumthor schichtete insgesamt 60.000 Valser Quarzitplatten aufeinander und schuf so eine Art Museum für die mineralhaltigen Quellen, die hier unter der Erde entspringen. Die Badegäste betreten die Therme durch einen unterirdischen Tunnel und dringen so tief in das Herz des Berges vor. Dort wartet die Garderobe, die auf eine Galerie hinausgeht. Auf der darunter gelegenen Hauptebene befinden sich sechs Pools, deren Wassertemperatur von eiskalt bis kochend heiß reicht. Im Eisbad klettert die Quecksilbersäule gerade mal bis auf 14°C, während im Feuerbad stolze 42°C erreicht werden. Gemäßigter ist das Blütenbad voll duftender Blütenblätter, in dem angenehme 33°C herrschen. Unter den in den Fels eingelassenen Bädern liegen die silbern gestrichenen Behandlungsräume. Dort werden zahlreiche Anwendungen wie Aroma-, Thalassotherapie und Massagen angeboten. Passend zu den Quarzitplatten ist das Wellness-Special eine Stone-Massage: Knapp zwei Stunden lang lässt der Therapeut heiße, in Aromaöl getränkte Kiesel über den Körper gleiten und löst so sämtliche Verspannungen. Laut den Besitzern, soll auch das Spa-eigene 140-Betten-Hotel bald dem Niveau der Therme Vals entsprechen.

WELLNESS-SPECIAL: STONE-MASSAGE

Les Thermes Vals prennent le contre-pied de l'architecture alpine traditionnelle ; pourtant, cet édifice monumental s'intègre parfaitement au paysage. Peter Zumthor, l'architecte, a disposé 60 000 blocs de quartzite pour créer un lieu digne des eaux minérales venues du sous-sol. Un tunnel s'enfonce comme vers le cœur de la montagne et mène aux vestiaires qui surplombent les bassins – six piscines dans lesquelles la température de l'eau s'échelonne de glaciale – 14°C – à très chaud – 42°C, parfait pour se détendre. Entre les deux, le bassin de fleurs – une eau pleine de pétales parfumés, maintenue à 33°C. Sous les bassins et leur décor d'eau et de roche, les salles de soins peintes en gris argent servent de cadre à des traitements qui comprennent soins de beauté, aromathérapie, thalassothérapie et massages. Comme en écho aux murs de quartzite, le soin phare du spa est un massage aux pierres. Pendant près de deux heures, le masseur effleure le corps de galets chauds enduits d'huiles aromatiques au contact desquels les tensions s'évanouissent. Les propriétaires assurent que bientôt, l'hôtel de 140 chambres pourra rivaliser avec le raffinement du Spa.

SOIN PHARE : MASSAGE AUX PIERRES

Therme Vals
7132 Vals
Switzerland

TEL: +41 81 9268961
FAX: +41 81 9268000
EMAIL: therme@therme-vals.ch
WEBSITE: www.therme-vals.ch

Çemberlitaş Bath

When Çemberlitaş Bath first opened, Murat III. reigned over the Ottoman Empire. That was back in 1584, and the hammam remains as vital to the city's social fabric as it was so many centuries ago. Mimar Sinan, the legendary architect of the Süleymaniye, designed the majestic marble edifice. As is customary, the interior is divided into separate sections for men and women. Upon entering, clothing and personal belongings are stowed in lockers and replaced with the accoutrements of the traditional Turkish bathing ritual: pestemals (raw cotton wraps for modesty), slippers, towels, soap, and shampoo. So equipped, visitors proceed to an imposing, marble-lined chamber whose grandeur reflects the almost religious solemnity of the cleansing rite. Under a domed ceiling pierced with honeycombs of light, a heated marble platform invites repose – a literal warm-up to the rigorous rubdown. The routine begins with a thorough exfoliation. After covering the body with a sudsy mixture, your masseur or masseuse vigorously scrubs off layers of dead skin with a rough mitt. An energetic top-to-toe massage follows – long, deep strokes and firm kneading leave the body utterly relaxed. After a warm-water rinse, a shampoo with scalp massage and a restorative glass of mint tea reawaken the psyche in preparation for re-entry into Istanbul's intricacies.

SIGNATURE TREATMENT: HAMMAM

Als das Çemberlitaş-Bad seine Pforten öffnete, herrschte noch Murat III. über das Osmanische Reich. Das war 1584, doch seitdem hat der Hamam für die Einwohner Istanbuls keineswegs an Bedeutung verloren. Entworfen wurde der Marmorbau von Mimar Sinan, dem legendären Architekt der Süleymaniye. Im Innern des Gebäudes befinden sich traditionsgemäß zwei strikt voneinander getrennte Bereiche: einer für Männer und einer für Frauen. Nach dem Betreten des Bades schließt man Kleider und persönliche Gegenstände in einen Spind und erhält im Gegenzug alles, was man für das türkische Baderitual benötigt: Peştemal (ein grobes Baumwolltuch, mit dem man seine Blöße bedeckt), Badesandalen, Handtücher, Seife und Shampoo. Dementsprechend versorgt, geht man in einen imposanten, marmorvertäfelten Raum, dessen Grandezza den feierlichen, ja fast schon religiösen Ernst des Reinigungsrituals widerspiegelt. Unter der Kuppel mit den kleinen Lichtöffnungen lädt ein beheiztes Marmorpodest zum Entspannen ein – genau das Richtige, um sich für die nun folgende Rubbelmassage „aufzuwärmen". Die Behandlung beginnt mit einem gründlichen Peeling. Dazu schäumt einen der Masseur bzw. die Masseurin von Kopf bis Fuß ein und entfernt die abgestorbenen Hautzellen mit einem Luffahandschuh. Es folgt eine belebende Ganzkörpermassage, bei der man so lange durchgeknetet wird, bis der Körper völlig entspannt ist. Nach Warmwassergüssen, einer Haarwäsche inklusive Kopfhautmassage und einem Glas Minztee fühlt man sich erfrischt und bereit, wieder in das Istanbuler Gassengewirr hinauszutreten.

WELLNESS-SPECIAL: HAMAM

Le sultan Murat III. régnait sur l'empire ottoman lorsque furent fondés les bains de Çemberlitaş, en 1584. Aujourd'hui comme hier, ils occupent une place centrale dans vie sociale d'Istanbul. Mimar Sinan, le célèbre architecte de la Süleymaniye, en a conçu les majestueux édifices de marbre. Selon la coutume, l'intérieur est divisé en sections séparées pour les hommes et les femmes. À l'entrée, on quitte ses vêtements pour la tenue traditionnelle : peştemal (pagnes de coton) et mules. Équipé de serviette, de savon et de shampooing, on accède à une vaste salle toute en marbre, dont la splendeur rappelle que le hammam comporte une dimension presque religieuse. Sous une coupole percée de rais de lumière, une plateforme de marbre chauffée invite au repos et prépare aux vigoureuses frictions qui suivent. Le corps enduit d'un produit savonneux, le masseur – ou la masseuse – frotte avec un gant spécial, pour éliminer les cellules mortes. Ensuite, un massage de tout le corps détend et relaxe grâce à des pressions longues et fermes. Le rinçage à l'eau chaude est suivi d'un shampooing, d'un massage du crâne et d'un thé à la menthe qui prépare l'esprit à retrouver l'agitation d'Istanbul.

SOIN PHARE: HAMMAM

Çemberlitaş Bath
Verzirhan Cad. No. 8
34440 Çemberlitaş
Istanbul, Turkey

TEL: +90 212 5227974
FAX: +90 212 5112535
EMAIL: contact@cemberlitashamami.com.tr
WEBSITE: www.cemberlitashamami.com.tr

Harrogate
Turkish Baths & Health Spa

In the heart of Harrogate, a genteel and historic spa town in the north of England, Eastern and Western approaches to taking the waters converge at the Turkish Baths – a recently refurbished landmark that first opened its doors in 1897. Within, the Victorian sobriety of dark, richly polished woodwork meets the Eastern excess of ceilings painted in fanciful arabesques, multicolored terrazzo floors, and walls lined with mosaic tiles laid in geometric patterns – all meticulously repaired and restored. And the menu of treatments similarly offers the best of both worlds. Reflexology, Japanese reiki, and Swedish massage are among the many soothing ways to unwind, and East Indian head massage takes a gentle approach to relaxation with tender, fingertip strokes caressing scalp, face, and neck. But it's the Turkish baths that are the spa's raison d'être. The two-and-a-half-hour hammam ritual begins with a brisk shower. Next, the steam room's eucalyptus vapors ease tension and relax the body. From there, it's on to the bracing plunge pool, lined with tropical potted palms and filled with arctic water. Back to warmth in a sizzling excursion through three hot rooms that range from the Tepidarium's 120°F to the Laconium, where temperatures soar to 220°F. Finally, the misleadingly named Frigidarium offers a temperate segue between Turkish tradition and the Western world.

SIGNATURE TREATMENT: TURKISH BATH

Im Herzen von Harrogate, einem freundlichen, historischen Kurort im Norden Englands treffen im türkischen Dampfbad westliche und östliche Wellness-Spezialitäten aufeinander. Das unter Denkmalschutz stehende Gebäude, das seine Pforten erstmals im Jahr 1897 öffnete, wurde erst kürzlich originalgetreu restauriert. In seinem Innern vereint sich das dunkle, polierte Holz aus Viktorianischen Zeiten mit der ganzen Pracht des Orients: Die Decken sind mit bunten Ornamenten geschmückt, geometrische Mosaike zieren Terrazzoboden und Wände. Auch die Anwendungen bieten das Beste aus Ost und West: Reflexologie, japanisches Reiki und Schwedische Massage sind nur einige von vielen Möglichkeiten, sich zu entspannen. Wer es etwas sanfter mag, entscheidet sich für die Indische Kopfmassage, bei der Kopfhaut, Gesicht und Nacken behutsam gestreichelt werden. Das Verlockendste ist jedoch ein Besuch des Türkischen Dampfbads. Das zweieinhalbstündige Hamam-Ritual beginnt mit einer kurzen Dusche. Danach geht es zum Entspannen in den mit Eukalyptus bedufteten Dampfraum und schließlich ins Tauchbecken. Letzteres wird von Palmen gesäumt und enthält eiskaltes Wasser, das für eine kurze Erfrischung sorgt. Danach sucht man die Wärme in den drei aufeinander folgenden Räumen mit Temperaturen zwischen 48°C (Tepidarium) und 104°C (Laconium). Den Abschluss bildet ein Aufenthalt in dem irreführend benannten Frigidarium: Hier herrscht eine durchweg angenehme Temperatur, eine Art Mittelding zwischen türkischer Tradition und der westlichen Welt.

WELLNESS-SPECIAL: TÜRKISCHES DAMPFBAD

Au cœur de Harrogate, ville d'eau raffinée du Nord de l'Angleterre, les traditions orientales et occidentales se sont unies pour créer les Turkish Baths («bains turcs») – véritable institution fondée en 1897 et récemment rénovée. À l'intérieur, la sobriété des boiseries victoriennes, vernies et sombres, offre un contrepoint surprenant et harmonieux à la richesse toute orientale des plafonds décorés d'arabesques subtiles, aux sols de terrazzo multicolore, aux mosaïques murales, tous parfaitement restaurés. De la même façon, les soins offerts réunissent le meilleur des deux cultures. Parmi d'autres, réflexologie, reiki japonais et massages suédois permettent de se détendre tout en douceur, les massages des Indes libèrent des tensions grâce à des effleurements du crâne, du visage et du cou. Mais la raison d'être du spa sont les bains turcs. La séance rituelle au hammam dure deux heures et demie, et commence par une douche revigorante. Ensuite, les vapeurs d'eucalyptus détendent les muscles et apaisent l'esprit. L'eau glacée, dans la piscine entourée de palmiers en pots, apporte tonus et énergie avant de retrouver la chaleur de trois salles, du tepidarium à 48°C jusqu'au laconium et ses 104°C. Le frigidarium au nom trompeur permet une transition en douceur entre la chaleur des bains turcs et le monde occidental.

SOIN PHARE: BAINS TURCS

Harrogate Turkish Baths & Health Spa
Royal Baths
Parliament Street
Harrogate HG1 2WH, United Kingdom

TEL: +44 1423 556746
FAX: +44 1423 556760
EMAIL: info@harrogate.gov.uk
WEBSITE: www.harrogate.co.uk/turkishbaths

North America

Willow Stream Spa
at the Fairmont Banff Springs

A Scottish baronial castle served as inspiration for the historic Fairmont Banff Springs, whose majestic setting – in the heart of the Canadian Rockies – is one of its greatest assets. Opened in 1888 by the visionary general manager of the Canadian Pacific Railway, the 770-room hotel features furnishings that are replicas of original pieces from European castles and manor houses. The 35,000-square-foot Willow Stream Spa overlooks a sweeping vista of sky, mountains, and rolling valleys. The centerpiece is a strikingly designed therapeutic mineral pool, rich with Hungarian Thermal Mineral Kur, graced with an underwater speaker system, and surrounded by three cascading waterfall massage pools. (A 15-minute soak is recommended before treatments.) A 105-foot indoor heated saltwater swimming pool and 65-foot outdoor lap pool are also on hand, as are private steam rooms, whirlpools, sun terraces, and fireplace lounges. Treatments include the 120-minute Ultimate Ascent, which begins with a cup of herbal mountain tea and a warm aromatic footbath before a dry-brush exfoliation, massage, and wrap. The hour-long Rockies Rehydration is the ideal way to rejuvenate after a day out on the slopes: healing algae is blended with aloe vera and essential oils and applied to the skin.

SIGNATURE TREATMENT: ULTIMATE ASCENT

Ein schottisches Schloss diente als Vorbild für das historische Fairmont Banff Springs, dessen Lage im Herzen der kanadischen Rocky Mountains einfach atemberaubend ist. Das 1888 vom visionären Generaldirektor der Canadian Pacific Railways eröffnete Hotel mit 700 Zimmern ist stolz auf seine Stilmöbel, originalgetreue Repliken von Antiquitäten aus europäischen Schlössern und Herren-häusern. Vom über 3.250 Quadratmeter großen Willow-Stream-Spa hat man einen herrlichen Blick auf das beeindruckende Gebirgs-panorama. Sein Prunkstück ist ein wunderschön geformter therapeutischer Pool, dessen Wasser mit einer ungarischen Thermal-Mineralkur angereichert ist. Der Pool verfügt über Unterwasser-Lautsprecher und wird von drei Wasserfall-Massage-Pools gesäumt. (Vor den Anwendungen wird ein 15-minütiges Tauchbad empfohlen.) Ein 32 Meter langes, beheiztes Meerwasser-Hallenbad sowie ein 20 Meter langes Außenbecken sind ebenfalls vorhanden, außerdem private Dampfräume, Whirlpools, Sonnenterrassen und Kaminzimmer. Zu den Anwendungen gehört das 120-minütige Wellness-Special „Ultimate Ascent", das mit einer Tasse Bergkräuter-tee und einem warmen Aroma-Fußbad beginnt. Anschließend folgen Bürstenpeeling, Massage und Bodywrap. Die einstündige „Rocky Rehydration" ist die ideale Verjüngungskur nach einem Tag auf der Skipiste: Heilende Algen, gemischt mit Aloe Vera und essenziellen Ölen, geben der Haut Feuchtigkeit zurück.

WELLNESS-SPECIAL: ULTIMATE ASCENT

Inspiré d'un château de style écossais, l'hôtel Fairmont Banff Springs est situé en plein cœur des montagnes Rocheuses canadiennes dans un cadre naturel majestueux. Ouvert en 1888 par le directeur général visionnaire de la compagnie Canadian Pacific Railway, l'hôtel avec 700 chambres est meublé de répliques de pièces provenant de châteaux et de manoirs européens. D'une superficie de 3 250 mètres carrés, le spa Willow Stream offre une vue panoramique sur les montagnes et les vallées environnantes. À l'intérieur, la piscine d'eau thermale surprend par son design : elle est équipée d'un système d'enceintes sous-marines et entourée de trois piscines à remous avec cascade d'eau minérale. (Un bain d'un quart d'heure est recommandé avant tout traitement.) L'établissement dispose également d'une piscine intérieure d'eau de mer chauffée de 32 mètres, d'une piscine extérieure de 20 mètres, de saunas individuels, de bains à remous, de terrasses et de salons avec cheminée. L'un des soins proposé est l'Ascension suprême, d'une durée de deux heures, qui commence par un bain de pieds chaud et aromatique accompagné d'une tasse d'infusion aux herbes de montagne. Le trai-tement se poursuit par une exfoliation à la brosse sèche, un massage et un enveloppement corporel. Quant à la Réhydratation des Rocheuses, elle constitue le moyen idéal pour régénérer la peau après une journée à la montagne : des algues pures sont mélangées à de l'aloe vera et des huiles essentielles, et le tout est ensuite appliqué sur la peau.

SOIN PHARE: ASCENSION SUPRÊME

Willow Stream Spa at the Fairmont Banff Springs
405 Spray Avenue
Banff, Alberta T1L 1J4
Canada

TEL: +1 403 7622211
FAX: +1 403 7625755
EMAIL: banffsprings@fairmont.com
WEBSITE: www.fairmont.com

King Pacific Lodge

For those who seek relaxation not in sun and sand but in the wilderness, there are few better destinations than the King Pacific Lodge on Princess Royal Island with its 17 spacious accommodations. After a full day of fishing, hiking, and kayaking in the glorious Pacific Northwest – or even after a full day spent doing not much more than reading and watching the clouds glide by – the spa at the King Pacific Lodge is a real treat. Built with fir with driftwood accents and mossy green hues for the walls, the spa brings to mind both the land and the ocean. Here, in the solitude of British Columbia's sparkling wilderness, a range of treatments inspired by the natural environment are on offer, such as the Canadian Moor Mud Body Wrap and the Wolf Track Hot Stone Wrap, which begins with a Swedish massage to awaken the senses and is followed by a cocoon-wrap with 67 wolf track basalt stones placed on tension and chakra points. The spa also has a sauna, steam bath, plunge pool, and Jacuzzi – perfect for winding down from the robust activities available at the lodge, which range from fly fishing to "spirit bear" excursions. For true lovers of marine life, this premier floating wilderness lodge offers guests the opportunity to spend a day with whale researchers at an orca lab or experience the wonder of the British Columbia salmon run.

SIGNATURE TREATMENT: CANADIAN MOOR MUD BODY WRAP

Für alle, die sich nicht am Strand sonnen, sondern in der Wildnis erholen wollen, ist das King Pacific Lodge auf Princess Royal Island mit seinen 17 großzügig angelegten Unterkünften geradezu ideal. Wer tagsüber wandert, angelt, auf dem herrlichen Nordwestpazifik Kajak fährt oder einfach nur faulenzt, liest und den Wolken nachsieht, lässt sich abends gern im hauseigenen Spa verwöhnen. Mit seinen moosgrünen Wänden ist das aus Fichten- und zum Teil aus Treibholz erbaute Spa eine Reminiszenz an Land und Meer. In der einsamen Wildnis von British Columbia werden gleich mehrere, von der Natur inspirierte Behandlungen wie der kanadische Moorschlamm-Bodywrap oder der „Wolf-Track-Hot-Stone-Wrap" angeboten. Letzterer beginnt mit einer belebenden Schwedischen Massage, gefolgt von einem Spezialwickel, bei dem 67 Basaltsteine auf wichtige Spannungs- und Chakra-Punkte aufgelegt und mit Baumwollbandagen fixiert werden. Darüber hinaus verfügt das Spa über Sauna, Dampfbad, Tauchbecken und Jacuzzi – ein idealer Ausgleich für die vom Hotel angebotenen Outdoor-Aktivitäten, die vom Fliegenfischen bis hin zu Grislibär-Exkursionen reichen. Liebhabern der Meeresfauna bietet die schwimmende Luxus-Lodge an, einen Tag mit den Walforschern des Orka-Labs zu verbringen oder das für British Columbia typische Naturschauspiel der Lachswanderung zu bewundern.

WELLNESS-SPECIAL: KANADISCHER MOORSCHLAMM-BODYWRAP

Pour ceux qui souhaitent se relaxer en pleine nature, et non sur le sable de plages ensoleillées, rien de tel qu'un séjour au King Pacific Lodge sur l'île de la Princesse-Royale dans un de ses 17 logements spacieux. Après une journée de pêche, de randonnée pédestre ou de kayak dans les paysages somptueux du Pacific Northwest, ou simplement après une journée dédiée uniquement à la lecture ou à regarder passer les nuages, le spa du King Pacific Lodge est un vrai plaisir. Bâti en sapin, avec des murs aux couleurs rappelant le bois flotté et le vert de la mousse, il évoque à la fois la terre et l'océan. Là, dans la solitude de la nature chatoyante de la Colombie-Britannique, une grande variété de traitements, directement inspirés de l'environnement naturel, est proposée, comme l'enveloppement corporel à la boue ou le cocon aux pierres chaudes de Wolf Track Beach, qui commence par un massage suédois pour réveiller les sens et se poursuit par un cocon composé de 67 pierres de basalte disposées sur les points de tension et les chakras. L'établissement dispose également d'un sauna, d'un bain de vapeur, d'une piscine et d'un jacuzzi – idéal pour se détendre après avoir profité des nombreuses activités proposées, de la pêche à la mouche aux excursions d'observation des ours. Pour les amoureux de la vie marine, le King Pacific Lodge offre la possibilité de passer une journée en compagnie de spécialistes des baleines dans un laboratoire spécialisé ou de découvrir la migration des saumons.

SOIN PHARE: ENVELOPPEMENT CORPOREL À LA BOUE

King Pacific Lodge
255 West 1st Street, Suite 214
North Vancouver, BC V7M 3G8
Canada

TEL: +1 604 9875452
FAX: +1 604 9875472
EMAIL: info@kingpacificlodge.com
WEBSITE: www.kingpacificlodge.com

Sanctuary on Camelback Mountain

Asian spirituality meets the Arizona desert at this chic resort oasis, a former tennis ranch dating from the 1960s. The resort's 24 new casitas, decorated in minimalist splendor, surround the expansive infinity-edge pool, while 74 older, more traditional, casitas have more discreet settings up the mountain. The 12,000-square-foot, indoor/outdoor spa opened in January 2002. The cathedral-like reception area has soaring ceilings and a dramatic floor-to-ceiling window with mountain views. Eleven treatment rooms open onto an interior courtyard with a meditation garden and reflecting pool. In keeping with the spa's Eastern philosophy, signature treatments include the Sumatra coconut polish (in which fresh coconut is used to buff away dead skin cells) and a Thai foot massage (in which a wooden dowel is used with traditional reflexology). Most treatments can be performed in Sanctum, a private treatment suite for two with its own plunge pool, fire pit, and outdoor shower. There's also a 25-yard lap pool, a heated watsu pool, and a state-of-the-art fitness center. At night, Elements restaurant serves fare that's several notches above your average spa cuisine, and the adjoining Jade Bar plays host to a good-looking crowd of locals. In the shadow of Camelback's famous Praying Monk, the effect is appropriately serene.

SIGNATURE TREATMENT: SUMATRA COCONUT POLISH

In dieser eleganten Urlaubsoase, einem ehemaligen Tennishotel aus den 1960er Jahren, gehen asiatische Spiritualität und die Wüste Arizonas eine gelungene Verbindung ein. 24 neu errichtete Casitas in minimalistischem Stil umringen einen riesigen Naturpool, während die 74 älteren, eher traditionell eingerichteten Bungalows etwas versteckter am Hang liegen. Das Spa mit 1.000 Quadratmetern Innen- und Außenfläche wurde im Januar 2002 eröffnet. Der Rezeptionsbereich erinnert mit seiner hohen Decke an eine Kathedrale. Panoramafenster bieten eine fantastische Aussicht auf die Berge. Die elf Behandlungsräume umschließen einen Innenhof mit Meditationsgarten und Pool. Passend zur fernöstlichen Philosophie dieses Spa werden Behandlungen angeboten wie das „Sumatra Coconut Polish", wo frisches Kokosnussfleisch abgestorbene Hautzellen entfernt, oder die Thai Fußmassage, einer traditionellen Reflexzonenmassage mit Rundholzstab. Fast alle Anwendungen kann man auch im Sanctum nutzen. Diese speziell für Paare gedachte Suite ist mit Tauchbecken, Feuerstelle und Außendusche ausgestattet. Darüber hinaus verfügt die Anlage über ein 23-Meter-Schwimmbecken, einen beheizten Watsu-Pool sowie über ein perfekt ausgestattetes Fitnesscenter. Abends diniert man vorzüglich im hauseigenen Restaurant. In der angrenzenden Jade Bar treffen sich die Reichen und Schönen der Gegend. Kurz gesagt: Vor der berühmten Kulisse des „Betenden Mönchs", einer Felsformation am Camelback Mountain, lässt es sich hervorragend entspannen.

WELLNESS-SPECIAL: SUMATRA COCONUT POLISH

La spiritualité asiatique et le désert de l'Arizona se rencontrent dans cette superbe oasis, ancien club de tennis datant des années 1960. Les 24 nouveaux bungalows, à la décoration sobre mais luxueuse, entourent l'immense piscine tandis que les 74 bungalows plus anciens et plus traditionnels sont situés dans un cadre discret sur fond de montagne. S'étendant en intérieur et en extérieur sur plus de 1 000 mètres carrés, le spa a ouvert ses portes en janvier 2002. La réception, aux plafonds vertigineusement hauts, fait penser à une cathédrale et une incroyable baie vitrée allant du sol au plafond offre une vue imprenable sur la montagne. Onze salles de soins donnent sur une cour intérieure avec un jardin de méditation et un bassin. S'inspirant des philosophies orientales, le spa propose des soins comme le polissage corporel à la noix de coco de Sumatra (la noix de coco fraîche est utilisée pour éliminer les cellules mortes) et le massage des pieds à la thaïlandaise (une cheville en bois est associée à la réflexologie traditionnelle). La plupart des soins peuvent être effectués dans la suite privée Sanctum pour deux personnes. Celle-ci est équipée d'une piscine individuelle, d'un foyer et d'une douche extérieure. Le spa dispose également d'une piscine de 23 mètres, d'une piscine chauffée pour le watsu et d'un centre de fitness ultramoderne. Le soir, le restaurant Elements propose des mets succulents tandis que le Jade Bar voisin accueille une foule de gens du pays. Dans l'ombre du célèbre Praying Monk de Camelback se dégage une sérénité de circonstance.

SOIN PHARE: POLISSAGE À LA NOIX DE COCO DE SUMATRA

Sanctuary on Camelback Mountain
5700 East McDonald Drive
Paradise Valley, AZ 85253
United States

TEL: +1 480 9482100
FAX: +1 480 4837314
EMAIL: info@sanctuaryaz.com
WEBSITE: www.sanctuaryaz.com

Calistoga Ranch

Calistoga, in California's Napa Valley, is renowned for its mud and water. Indeed, the tiny town has made its reputation by devising creative combinations of those two elements for the benefit of visitors' health and wellbeing. The small hotels and spas that administered these treatments tended to be "no frills", however – until Calistoga Ranch came along. Located on 157 acres in an oak tree-filled canyon, Calistoga Ranch comprises 46 luxurious guest lodges and an architectural vibe that is quintessentially Californian. The spa, known as the Bathhouse, nestles in the woods at the top of the canyon and features a Healing Waters Soaking Pool and beautifully appointed treatment rooms, each of which has an outdoor shower and soaking tub. The treatments are enriched by the famous local mud; the signature Calistoga Ranch Mud Wrap, for example, combines the detoxifying effects of mud with ache-relieving eucalyptus. Napa Valley's world-famous wine makes it way into spa specialties like the Vineyard Crush exfoliation, but visitors would be remiss if they did not experience the grapes the old-fashioned way at the thousands of wineries within a 20-mile radius of the property – or, more conveniently, on the deck of the resort's Lakehouse restaurant.

SIGNATURE TREATMENT: CALISTOGA RANCH MUD WRAP

Calistoga im kalifornischen Napa Valley ist für seinen Heilschlamm und sein Heilwasser berühmt. Indem das kleine Städtchen beide Elemente geschickt zum Wohle der Gäste kombinierte, erwarb es sich beträchtliches Ansehen. Bisher waren die kleinen Hotels und Spas, die solche Anwendungen anboten, eher schlicht – bis die Calistoga Ranch aufmachte. Das 157 Morgen große Anwesen liegt in einem mit Eichen bewachsenen Canyon und besteht aus 46 luxuriösen Gästehäusern im typisch kalifornischen Stil. Das Spa, „Bathhouse" genannt, versteckt sich in den Wäldern oben im Canyon und verfügt über einen Heilwasserpool sowie über wunderbar ausgestattete Behandlungsräume, die alle eine Außendusche und eine Badewanne besitzen. Die Anwendungen sind von dem Heilschlamm geprägt, für den die Gegend berühmt ist. Die Calistoga-Ranch-Schlammpackung zum Beispiel verbindet die entschlackende Wirkung des Schlamms mit dem schmerzlindernden Effekt von Eukalyptus. Der weltberühmte Wein aus Napa Valley hat zur Entwicklung von Spa-Specials wie dem Vineyard-Crush-Peeling beigetragen. Aber man verpasst etwas, wenn man die Trauben in den Tausenden von Weingütern, die sich im Umkreis von 30 km befinden, nicht auch auf ganz altmodische Art genießt – oder noch bequemer direkt auf der Terrasse des hauseigenen Lakehouse-Restaurants.

WELLNESS-SPECIAL: CALISTOGA-RANCH-SCHLAMMPACKUNG

Au cœur de la Napa Valley, en Californie, Calistoga est célèbre pour les vertus de son eau et de sa boue. En effet, la petite ville a bâti sa réputation sur l'élaboration d'ingénieux mélanges à partir de ces deux éléments pour le bien-être et la santé de ses visiteurs. Les petits hôtels et spas qui dispensaient ces soins étaient souvent sans prétention – jusqu'à la création du Calistoga Ranch. Situé sur un terrain de près de 65 hectares, dans un canyon planté de chênes, le Calistoga Ranch, à l'architecture typiquement californienne, abrite 46 chambres luxueuses. Le spa, connu sous le nom de The Bathhouse, est niché dans les bois en haut du canyon. Il dispose d'une piscine d'eau minérale, la Healing Waters Soaking Pool, et de salles de soins magnifiquement aménagées, chacune d'elles comportant une douche et une baignoire extérieures. Les soins sont élaborés à partir de la célèbre boue de la région. Ainsi, le soin phare de l'établissement, l'enveloppement corporel à la boue Calistoga Ranch, allie les effets détoxifiants de la boue aux propriétés analgésiques de l'eucalyptus. Le célèbre vignoble de la Napa Valley est également à l'honneur dans certaines spécialités du spa comme l'exfoliation aux grains de raisin écrasés. Et les visiteurs ne sauraient quitter le Calistoga Ranch sans avoir dégusté les vins locaux en faisant la tournée des milliers de producteurs de la région dans un rayon de 30 kilomètres autour de l'établissement, ou confortablement installés à la terrasse du restaurant Lakehouse du Calistoga Ranch.

SOIN PHARE: ENVELOPPEMENT CORPOREL À LA BOUE CALISTOGA RANCH

Calistoga Ranch
580 Lommel Road
Calistoga, CA 94515
United States

TEL: +1 707 2542820
FAX: +1 707 2542888
EMAIL: reservations@calistogaranch.com
WEBSITE: www.calistogaranch.com

Sagewater Spa

A minimalist oasis in the California desert, Sagewater Spa was given a second life by owners Rhoni Epstein and Cristina Pestana. The pair stripped a 1950s vintage motel of its midcentury excesses to create a Zen-like haven. Out went the brown nylon carpet, in came the sander to buff up the concrete floors, which now gleam a pale, mint green. The centerpiece pool stayed put; the seven surrounding studio apartments were newly decked out in white-on-white modernism. These self-contained units, complete with fully equipped kitchens, turn into personal spas as therapists and aestheticians make house calls. Guests may choose from a room-service menu that includes a range of massage techniques, hot stone treatments, aromatherapy, body wraps, skin-care, manicures, pedicures, and more. But the spring-fed pool is Sagewater's real reason for being. Desert substrata imbue the water with a cocktail of healing minerals while subterranean thermodynamics heat it to a sizzling 165°F. The water, cooled to a stress-dissolving 105° in the soaking section and a just-right 90°F in the swimming area, soothes aching joints and leaves your skin feeling silky. The surrounding, sage-scented landscape of swaying palms, coffee-colored hills, and mauve mountains nourishes the spirit – a desert reverie awash in California sunshine.

SIGNATURE TREATMENT: HEALING SPRING WATER

Die minimalistische Oase in der kalifornischen Wüste wurde von ihren Eigentümern Rhoni Epstein und Cristina Pestana zu neuem Leben erweckt. Dazu befreite das Paar das Motel aus den 1950er Jahren von altem Ballast und machte daraus ein Zen-artiges Paradies. Die braune Auslegeware verschwand und gab blanken Betonboden frei, der mit einer Schleifmaschine so auf Hochglanz poliert wurde, dass er nun in einem blassen Minzton erstrahlt. Was blieb, waren der Pool im Zentrum der Anlage sowie die sieben umliegenden Studio-Apartments, die jetzt sehr modernistisch ganz in Weiß gehalten sind. Die eigenständigen Apartments verfügen über komplett eingerichtete Küchen. Wenn die Therapeuten und Kosmetikerinnen kommen, verwandeln sie sich sogar in ein privates Spa. Die Gäste können aus einem Room-Service-Angebot auswählen, das Massagen, Behandlungen mit heißen Steinen, Aromatherapie, Bodywraps, Hautpflege, Maniküre und Pediküre beinhaltet. Am berühmtesten ist das Sagewater für seinen Quellwasser-Pool. Wüstensubstrate reichern das Wasser mit einem Cocktail aus heilenden Mineralien an, während es die unterirdische Thermodynamik auf 74°C aufheizt. Dieses Wasser, das im Badebereich auf 40°C und im Schwimmbereich auf angenehme 32°C heruntergekühlt wird, lindert Gelenkschmerzen und macht die Haut seidig glatt. Der Salbeiduft, die Palmen, die kaffeebraunen Hügel und violetten Berge sind die reinste Wohltat für die Seele – eine von der kalifornischen Sonne durchflutete Wüstenträumerei.

WELLNESS-SPECIAL: HEILENDES QUELLWASSER

Petite oasis au milieu du désert californien, le Sagewater Spa connaît une seconde jeunesse grâce à ses propriétaires Rhoni Epstein et Cristina Pestana. Le couple a remodelé un vieux motel de 1950 pour créer un havre de paix d'inspiration zen. Les tapis marron en nylon ont laissé la place aux sols polis en béton qui, aujourd'hui, brillent d'un vert menthe pâle. La piscine centrale est restée en place tandis que les sept studios qui l'entourent ont été redécorés dans un style moderne en blanc sur blanc. Ces logements indépendants, équipés de cuisines entièrement aménagées, se transforment en véritables spas individuels lorsque thérapeutes et esthéticiennes font des visites à domicile. Les hôtes peuvent choisir: massages, soins aux pierres chaudes, aromathérapie, enveloppements corporels, soin de la peau, manucure, pédicure, etc. Néanmoins, le joyau de l'établissement reste sa piscine d'eau de source. Le sous-sol du désert enrichit l'eau avec de nombreux minéraux tandis que les phénomènes thermodynamiques souterrains la chauffent à plus de 74°C. Cette eau, refroidie à 40°C dans le bain réservé à la relaxation et à 32°C dans la partie réservée à la nage, soulage les articulations douloureuses et laisse comme un voile soyeux sur la peau. Le paysage environnant nourri l'esprit, comme une rêverie solitaire loin du soleil de Californie.

SOIN PHARE: EAU DE SOURCE CURATIVE

Sagewater Spa
12689 Eliseo Road
Desert Hot Springs, CA 92240
United States

TEL: +1 760 2201554
FAX: +1 760 2511553
EMAIL: sagewater.spa@verizon.net
WEBSITE: www.sagewaterspa.com

The Golden Door

The renowned Golden Door Spa with 50 rooms has been around since 1958 and recently expanded to include men's weeks and co-ed weeks several times a year. The spa places a lot of effort in maintaining its beautiful country surroundings and keeping the estate beautiful. The Golden Door takes particular pride in both the spa's natural assets, like the colorful camellias and fuchsia that grow over the site, and its man-made beauties within its million-dollar art and antiques collection. This attention stretches to every part of the Golden Door experience – even the spa's entrance gate is bedecked with jewels. Especially impressive are the rare antique lanterns that guests find while exploring the property. The Golden Door takes advantage of its secluded southern California location to give guests ample space to relax and rejuvenate. The Dragon Tree Gym and the Beauty Court are stocked with two swimming pools, tennis courts, and a private hiking hillside. The spa also has an impressive bathhouse with a unique fan-shaped therapy pool and private rooms for wraps and scrubs. The Golden Door has its own line of skin-care products, which are available at the spa and sold worldwide. The spa's signature treatment is a facial that starts with an exfoliating pineapple scrub, then mists the face with essence of orange. The treatment finishes with an oxygen facial masque and a Golden C Serum Treatment that improves circulation.

SIGNATURE TREATMENT: PINEAPPLE SCRUB/GOLDEN C SERUM TREATMENT

Das renommierte Golden Door Spa mit 50 Zimmern existiert bereits seit 1958 und bietet seit kurzem auch Kuren für Männer und Paare an. Das Spa investiert viel in die Pflege seiner wunderschönen Gartenanlage. Und so ist man mit Recht auf die bunten Kamelien und Fuchsien genauso stolz wie auf die millionenschwere Kunst- und Antiquitätensammlung. Alles ist bis ins letzte Detail durchgestylt. Beeindruckend sind auch die ungewöhnlich geformten, antiken Laternen, auf die man bei der Erkundung des Geländes stößt. Das idyllisch gelegene Golden Door bietet seinen Gästen jede Menge Platz zum Entspannen. Dragon-Tree-Gym und Beauty Court verfügen über zwei Swimming Pools, Tennisplätze und einen privaten Wanderweg. Das Spa besitzt zudem ein eindrucksvolles Badehaus mit dem einzigartigen Therapie-Pool in Form eines Fächers sowie private Behandlungsräumen für Wraps und Peelings. Das Golden Door hat eine eigene Pflegeserie, die im Spa erhältlich ist und weltweit verkauft wird. Das Wellness-Special ist eine Gesichtsbehandlung, die mit einem Ananas-Peeling beginnt. Danach wird das Gesicht mit Orangen-Essenz eingesprüht. Den Abschluss bilden eine Sauerstoff-Gesichtsmaske sowie das durchblutungsfördernde „Golden-C-Serum-Treatment".

WELLNESS-SPECIAL: ANANAS-SCRUB/GOLDEN-C-SERUM-TREATMENT

Créé en 1958, le célèbre Golden Door avec 50 chambres a récemment enrichi sa gamme de services et propose désormais des séjours pour hommes et des séjours mixtes plusieurs fois dans l'année. Le spa s'efforce de préserver la beauté naturelle de son environnement tout en améliorant la qualité de l'établissement. Il tire une fierté légitime de son environnement naturel – comment ne pas s'émerveiller devant les camélias et les fuchsias aux couleurs vives qui poussent sur le site ? – et de sa collection d'œuvres et d'objets d'art. Ce souci de beauté est omniprésent, jusque dans les pierres précieuses qui ornent la porte d'entrée du spa. Extrêmement rares, les lanternes anciennes que le visiteur rencontre dans le domaine sont particulièrement remarquables. Le Golden Door profite de sa situation retirée au sud de la Californie pour offrir à ses hôtes de grands espaces pour se détendre et se ressourcer. Le Dragon Tree Gym et le Beauty Court sont équipés de deux piscines et de courts de tennis, et une colline privée est réservée à la randonnée. Le spa dispose également de bains impressionnants avec une piscine unique en forme d'éventail et des salles privées pour les enveloppements et les exfoliations. Le Golden Door possède sa propre ligne de produits de beauté, en vente sur le site même et dans le monde entier. Le soin phare est un soin du visage qui commence par une exfoliation à l'ananas et se poursuit par une vaporisation du visage à l'essence d'orange. Il se termine par un masque à base d'oxygène et un soin au sérum C qui favorise la circulation.

SOIN PHARE : GOMMAGE À L'ANANAS ET SOIN RÉGÉNÉRATEUR AU SÉRUM C

The Golden Door
PO Box 463077
Escondido, CA 92046
United States

TEL: +1 760 744 5777
FAX: +1 760 471 2393
EMAIL: reservations@goldendoor.com
WEBSITE: www.goldendoor.com

Hotel Healdsburg

The Hotel Healdsburg is an inviting minimalist retreat located in the heart of three of the world's premier wine appellations: Dry Creek Valley, the Russian River Valley, and Alexander Valley. Savoring a glass of perfect Zinfandel or Chardonnay by the light and warmth of the hotel's roaring fire is integral to the hotel experience, as is enjoying the seasonal cuisine served at the Charlie Palmer's Dry Creek Kitchen. Every last detail is addressed in the sophisticated 55 guest rooms: Frette linens, goose down duvets, luxurious soaking tubs, and Tibetan rugs. In the sleek spa, regenerative total body treatments provide the Healdsburg Experience: options include Drench, a hydrating body massage followed by a moisture-rich body wrap; Purify, a gentle dry brushing followed by a sea-weed wrap, an indulgent soak in the tub, and a full body massage; and Romance, a passion oil massage for two followed by a luxuriating soak in a heated tub and topped off by a glass of sparkling wine and a selection of chocolate truffles. Natural ingredients such as olive oil, green tea, and lemon are incorporated into face, body, feet, and hand treatments. Activities in the Healdsburg area include, of course, wine tasting, but also everything from hot air ballooning, to hiking, to golf.

SIGNATURE TREATMENT: HEALDSBURG EXPERIENCE

Das Healdsburg ist ein einladendes, minimalistisch eingerichtetes Hotel, das inmitten von drei weltberühmten Weinanbaugebieten liegt: Dry Creek Valley, Russian River Valley und Alexander Valley. Ein Abend am prasselnden Hotelkamin bei einem Glas erlesenen Zinfandels oder Chardonnays ist eine Erfahrung, die man sich nicht entgehen lassen sollte. Dasselbe gilt für den Besuch von Charlie Palmers Dry Creek Kitchen mit ihrer köstlichen saisonalen Küche. In den 55 eleganten Gästezimmern stimmt jedes Detail: Sie alle sind mit Frette-Bettwäsche, Daunendecken, luxuriösen Badewannen und tibetischen Teppichen ausgestattet. Im stilvollen Spa sorgen regenerierende Ganzkörperbehandlungen für die „Healdsburg Expericence": Der Gast hat die Wahl zwischen „Drench", einer feuchtigkeitsspendenden Massage, gefolgt von einem ebensolchen Bodywrap, oder „Purify", einer sanften Bürstenmassage, an die sich eine Algenpackung, ein köstliches Wannenbad und eine Ganzkörpermassage anschließen. „Romance" ist eine Anwendung speziell für Paare, die eine Massage mit Passionsfruchtöl, ein herrliches Bad in der heißen Wanne und ein Glas moussierenden Weins inklusive Trüffelpralinen umfasst. Gesicht, Körper, Füße und Hände werden mit natürlichen Zutaten wie Olivenöl, Grünem Tee und Zitrone verwöhnt. Natürlich bietet das Healdsburg auch Weinverkostungen oder Aktivitäten wie Heißluftballonfahrten, Wandern und Golfspielen an.

WELLNESS-SPECIAL: HEALDSBURG EXPERIENCE

L'Hôtel Healdsburg est un lieu de retraite sobre et attrayant, situé au point de rencontre de trois vignobles qui ont donné leur nom à trois grandes appellations : Dry Creek Valley, Russian River Valley et Alexander Valley. Déguster un verre de zinfandel ou de chardonnay devant le feu qui crépite dans la cheminée de l'hôtel fait partie des plaisirs du lieu, tout comme apprécier les mets de saison préparés par le Charlie Palmer's Dry Creek Kitchen. Dans les 55 chambres à l'élégance raffinée, une attention particulière est portée aux moindres détails : linge Frette, couettes en duvet d'oie, baignoires luxueuses et tapis tibétains. Dans le spa, « l'expérience Healdsburg » se compose d'une série de soins corporels régénérateurs : « l'immersion » (massage corporel hydratant suivi d'un enveloppement complet très humide), « la purification » (gommage doux à sec suivi d'un enveloppement aux algues, d'un bain régénérateur et d'un massage corporel complet) et « la romance » (massage pour deux à l'huile de fruit de la passion suivi d'un bon bain dans une baignoire chauffée avec un verre de vin pétillant et un assortiment de truffes au chocolat). Des ingrédients naturels comme l'huile d'olive, le thé vert et le citron entrent dans la composition des soins pour le visage, le corps, les pieds et les mains. L'Hôtel Healdsburg propose de nombreuses activités, dont la dégustation de vin, bien entendu, mais également le vol en montgolfière, la randonnée ou le golf.

SOIN PHARE : EXPÉRIENCE HEALDSBURG

Hotel Healdsburg
25 Matheson Street
Healdsburg, CA 95448
United States

TEL: +1 707 4312800
FAX: +1 707 4310414
EMAIL: frontoffice@hotelhealdsburg.com
WEBSITE: www.hotelhealdsburg.com

The Carneros Inn

In the heart of the Napa Valley's Carneros wine-making region lies the Carneros Inn. The 86 simple cottages tucked amid vineyards in this scenic area belie, at first glance, the luxury housed within. Heated private gardens, sumptuous linens, flat screen TVs, soaking tubs, outdoor showers, and fireplaces all make for an indulgent hideaway. Perched on a hill with a magnificent view of the Napa Valley is the Hilltop Dining Room, featuring French-inspired cuisine such as Pinot Noir braised short ribs and lobster stuffed monkfish filet. Just outside the restaurant's doors is the stunning infinity-edge pool and hot tub and the Inn's immaculate spa. Treatments at the spa are inspired by the land that surrounds it. Services utilize the bounty of indigenous plants and natural ingredients found in the Carneros region – from olives to mustard seed, grapeseed to goat butter – and are categorized accordingly: The Harvests, The Minerals, The Cellars, The Farms, and The Creeks of Carneros. The spa's signature Healing Gem and Stone Massage provides a nurturing full-body massage with solar-charged aromatherapy oils and smooth volcanic stones. At the close, seven semiprecious gems rest on essential chakra points down the center of your body, bringing body, mind, and spirit into balance.

SIGNATURE TREATMENT: CARNEROS HEALING GEM AND STONE MASSAGE

The Carneros Inn befindet sich in der gleichnamigen Weinregion im kalifornischen Napa Valley. Die idyllisch in den Weinbergen gelegenen 86 Cottages sind von innen wesentlich luxuriöser, als man von außen vermuten würde. Beheizbare Privatgärten, kostbare Bettwäsche, Flachbildfernseher, großzügige Badewannen, Freiluftduschen und ein eigener Kamin machen sie zu einem herrlichen Refugium. Hoch oben auf einem Hügel thront der Hilltop Dining Room. Von hier aus hat man einen herrlichen Blick über das Napa Valley. Auf der Speisekarte stehen von der französischen Küche inspirierte Gerichte wie in Pinot Noir geschmorte Short-Rib-Steaks oder Mönchsfischfilet mit Hummerfüllung. Direkt vor dem Restaurant stößt man auf einen prächtigen Naturpool, Heißwasserbecken und das Spa. Die angebotenen Behandlungen spiegeln die hiesige Landschaft wieder. Alle Anwendungen basieren auf einheimischen Pflanzen und anderen natürlichen Zutaten aus der Carneros-Region wie Oliven, Senfkörner, Traubenkerne oder Ziegenbutter. Dementsprechend heißen sie auch „The Harvests", „The Minerals", „The Cellars", „The Farms" und „The Creeks of Carneros". Das Wellness-Special des Spa, die Heilkristall- und Steinmassage umfasst eine pflegende Ganzkörpermassage mit Aromatherapie-Ölen und glattem vulkanischen Gestein. Zum Schluss werden sieben Halbedelsteine auf wichtige Chakrapunkte aufgelegt, um Körper und Geist ins Gleichgewicht zu bringen.

WELLNESS-SPECIAL: CARNEROS HEILKRISTALL- UND STEINMASSAGE

Au cœur du vignoble de Carneros dans la Napa Valley se trouve The Inn at Carneros. Perdues au milieu des vignes, les 86 villas, d'apparence modeste, cachent de luxeux intérieurs. Jardins privés chauffés, linge somptueux, téléviseurs à écran plat, baignoires luxueuses, douches extérieures et cheminées: autant d'éléments pour un bon petit nid douillet. Perché en haut d'une colline offrant une vue magnifique sur la Napa Valley, le Hilltop Dining Room propose des plats d'inspiration française comme la côte de bœuf braisée au pinot noir ou le homard farci aux filets de lotte. Juste à côté du restaurant se trouvent l'immense piscine et le jacuzzi, ainsi que le spa proprement dit. Les soins prodigués au spa s'inspirent de la nature environnante. Ils tirent parti de l'abondance des plantes indigènes et des ingrédients naturels présents dans la région de Carneros (olives, graines de moutarde, pépins de raisin, beurre de chèvre) et sont classés en différentes catégories: les Moissons, les Minéraux, les Caves, les Fermes et les Criques de Carneros. Le massage régénérateur aux pierres et pierres précieuses proposé par le spa est un massage corporel complet et nourrissant à base d'huiles aromatiques et de pierres volcaniques lisses. À la fin du soin, sept pierres semi-précieuses sont disposées sur les principaux chakras au centre du corps afin d'harmoniser le corps et l'esprit.

SOIN PHARE: MASSAGE RÉGÉNÉRATEUR AUX PIERRES ET PIERRES PRÉCIEUSES

The Carneros Inn
4048 Sonoma Highway
Napa, CA 94559
United States

TEL: +1 707 2994900
FAX: +1 707 2994950
EMAIL: info@thecarnerosinn.com
WEBSITE: www.thecarnerosinn.com

Ojai Valley Inn & Spa

"Heaven on earth" aptly describes the Spa Ojai – the surrounding valleys and bountiful gardens served as Shangri-La, the mythical paradise in Frank Capra's film, *Lost Horizon*. Today, this luxurious New Age retreat with its 65 guest rooms offers a range of sybaritic antidotes to the stresses of this century. The architecture reflects the Spanish Colonial tradition, with whitewashed walls, terracotta roofs, intricate ironwork, and a fifty-foot bell tower overlooking a central courtyard. Sunrise tai chi classes are held on the lawn or in airy studios in the Mind/Body Center, where yoga, aerobics, and art therapy are also on offer. Treatment rooms feature walls painted in warm earth tones. Some have a crackling fire within, a cozy accompaniment to such indulgences as an elderberry herbal wrap (all ingredients gathered from the nearby garden). A special domed room is reserved for the group practice of Kuyam, the spa's signature treatment. This traditional Native American purifying ritual begins with a mineral-rich mudpack. Herb-infused steam then fills the dome, saturating and perfuming the air during the guided meditation session that follows. A shower comes next, followed by an application of hydrating lotion and a warm linen wrap. So enveloped, take a seat on the loggia – an outdoor refuge from which to contemplate the heavenly panorama.

SIGNATURE TREATMENT: KUYAM

Das Spa Ojai ist wirklich der Himmel auf Erden – die umliegenden Täler und Felder fungierten einst als das geheimnisumwobene Paradies in Frank Capras Film *Die Fesseln von Shangri-La*. Heute bietet diese luxuriöse New-Age-Oase mit ihren 65 Gästezimmern eine ganze Reihe von paradiesischen Anwendungen, bei denen die Zeit stehen zu bleiben scheint. Die Architektur der strahlend weiß gestrichenen Anlage mit den Ziegeldächern, schmiedeeisernen Ornamenten, Glockenturm und zentralem Innenhof erinnert an den Stil spanischer Kolonialbauten. Bei Sonnenaufgang kann man an Tai-Chi-Kursen auf dem Rasen teilnehmen oder sich ins Mind/Body-Center begeben. Dort werden Yoga, Aerobic oder Kunsttherapie angeboten. Die Behandlungsräume sind in warmen Erdtönen gehalten. Manche besitzen sogar einen prasselnden Kamin – eine Atmosphäre, in der man sich nur zu gern von einem Holunderbeeren-Kräuterwickel verwöhnen lässt. (Alle Zutaten stammen aus dem Spa-eigenen Garten). Ein von einer Kuppel überwölbter Raum ist dem Wellness-Special „Kuyam" vorbehalten. Dieses in der Gruppe durchgeführte Reinigungsritual nach indianischer Tradition beginnt mit einer mineralhaltigen Schlammpackung. Anschließend füllen Kräuterdämpfe die Kuppel und reichern die Raumluft während der nun folgenden geführten Meditation mit ihrem Duft an. Danach warten eine Dusche und Baumwollwickel mit einer Feuchtigkeitslotion. So verpackt nimmt man auf der Loggia Platz und genießt das paradiesische Panorama.

WELLNESS-SPECIAL: KUYAM

Le spa Ojai est « Le paradis sur terre ». Les vallées environnantes et les jardins luxuriants ont servi de décor pour Shangri-La, le paradis mythique d'*Horizons perdus*, le film de Franck Capra. Aujourd'hui, ce luxueux refuge New Age avec 65 chambres propose une gamme d'antidotes sybaritiques contre les tensions de la vie moderne. L'architecture s'inspire du style colonial espagnol avec une tour de 15 mètres donnant sur une cour intérieure. Des cours de taï-chi ont lieu au lever du soleil sur la pelouse ou dans les salles lumineuses du Mind/Body Center, qui propose également des séances de yoga, d'aérobic et d'art-thérapie. Les murs des salles de soins sont peints dans de chaleureux tons ocre. Certaines possèdent une cheminée à l'intérieur, idéale pour se laisser aller à des douceurs comme un enveloppement aromatique aux baies de sureau (tous les ingrédients proviennent du jardin voisin). Une salle à coupole est réservée au Kuyam, soin phare de l'établissement prodigué en groupe. Pratiqué par les Indiens d'Amérique, ce rituel traditionnel de purification commence par un masque à l'argile riche en minéraux. Puis, un bain de vapeur aux herbes emplit toute la salle, parfumant et saturant l'air pendant la séance de méditation qui s'ensuit. Après une douche, le rituel se poursuit par l'application d'une lotion hydratante et un enveloppement chaud. Il n'y a plus qu'à prendre un siège sur la loggia pour admirer le merveilleux panorama.

SOIN PHARE: KUYAM

Ojai Valley Inn & Spa
905 Country Club Road
Ojai, CA 93023
United States

TEL: +1 805 6465511
FAX: +1 805 6467969
EMAIL: info@ojairesort.com
WEBSITE: www.ojairesort.com

Viceroy Palm Springs

Once a 1930s hideaway for the Hollywood set, the newly reborn Viceroy Palm Springs (formerly Estrella) is the embodiment of chic Palm Springs. Here, stark modern design contrasts with deeply theatrical elements to create a setting that's part resort, part movie set. Whippet statues line paths, lanterns sway next to beds in the 74 rooms, and chandeliers hang on curtained terraces. Interior designer Kelly Wearstler has a knack for creating memorable scenarios, and at the spa, lemon-yellow doors and crisp white surfaces provide a visually soothing counterpoint to the desert heat. The lounge is an irreverent take on the formal English Regency aesthetic, with white shag carpeting, framed stoneware pieces, a Grecian-inspired bust, and furnishings custom-designed by Wearstler. The holistic Dr. Hauschka line is the inspiration for the two-hour Dr. Hauschka facial, which requires a specially trained aesthetician. The Botanical Body Bliss uses a custom blend of fine European sea salts and African shea butter applied to the skin, followed by a Vichy shower and rub with a mixture of pure aloe juice and olive and evening primrose oils. Three pools, four outdoor massage cabanas and a massage room for couples with its own Jacuzzi terrace complete the picture.

SIGNATURE TREATMENT: BOTANICAL BODY BLISS WITH VICHY SHOWER

Das ehemalige Estrella, in dem sich in den 1930er Jahren halb Hollywood die Klinke in die Hand gab und das kürzlich unter dem Namen Viceroy Palm Springs neu eröffnet wurde, ist der letzte Schrei von Palm Springs: Hier bilden modernes Design und verspielte Elemente einen reizvollen Kontrast und schaffen ein Ambiente, das halb Hotel, halb Filmkulisse zu sein scheint. Windhundfiguren säumen die Wege, Laternen schwanken neben den Betten in den 74 Gästezimmern, und Kronleuchter schmücken Terrassen mit üppig drapierten Vorhängen. Die Innenarchitektin Kelly Wearstler weiß, wie man ein unvergessliches Szenario kreiert! Im Spa bilden die zitronengelben Türen und weißen Oberflächen einen kühlen Kontrast zur Hitze der Wüste. Die Lounge ist eine respektlose Interpretation des englischen Regency-Stils. Sie ist mit hellen, groben Wollteppichen, einer antikisierenden Büste sowie Möbeln, die Wearstler selbst entworfen hat, ausgestattet. Die ganzheitlich orientierte Dr.-Hauschka-Pflegeserie bildet die Grundlage für die gleichnamige Gesichtsbehandlung, die von einer speziell geschulten Kosmetikerin durchgeführt wird. Beim „Botanical Body Bliss" wird eine Spezialmischung aus europäischen Meersalzen und afrikanischer Kakaobutter aufgetragen, gefolgt von einer Vichy-Dusche sowie einem Peeling aus Aloe-Vera-Saft, Oliven- und Nachtkerzenöl. Drei Pools, vier halboffene Massage-Cabanas und ein Massage-Raum speziell für Paare mit eigener Jacuzzi-Terrasse runden das Angebot ab.

WELLNESS-SPECIAL: BOTANICAL BODY BLISS MIT VICHY-DUSCHE

Pied-à-terre des stars hollywoodiennes dans les années 1930, le nouveau Viceroy Palm Springs (anciennement Estrella) est aujourd'hui le symbole du Palm Springs chic. Là, un design résolument contemporain contraste avec des éléments tout droit sortis du monde du théâtre pour créer un décor qui relève à la fois du lieu de villégiature et du plateau de tournage. Des statues de lévriers jalonnent les allées, des lanternes se balancent près des lits dans les 74 chambres de l'hôtel et de grands lustres illuminent les terrasses garnies de rideaux. L'architecte d'intérieur Kelly Wearstler excelle dans la création de décors mémorables. Au spa, les portes jaune citron et les surfaces d'un blanc immaculé offrent un contraste visuel apaisant avec la chaleur du désert. Le salon rappelle le très formel style Régence anglais, avec des tapis blancs à longues franges, des céramiques, un buste d'inspiration grecque et des meubles créés par Wearstler pour l'occasion. Les produits du Dr Hauschka, qui propose une approche holistique des soins du corps, permettent la réalisation d'un masque (d'une durée de deux heures) que seule une esthéticienne spécialement formée peut effectuer. Le Bien-être botanique utilise un mélange maison de sels de mer fins d'Europe et de beurre de karité d'Afrique, que l'on applique sur la peau. Il se poursuit par une douche Vichy et un gommage à base de jus d'aloès pur, d'huile d'olive et d'huile d'onagre. Trois piscines, quatre cabines de massage extérieures et une salle de massage pour les couples avec jacuzzi en terrasse viennent compléter le tableau.

SOIN PHARE: BIEN-ÊTRE BOTANIQUE ET DOUCHE VICHY

Viceroy Palm Springs
415 South Belardo Road
Palm Springs, CA 92262
United States

TEL: +1 760 3204117
FAX: +1 760 3233303
EMAIL: info@viceroypalmsprings.com
WEBSITE: www.viceroypalmsprings.com

Spa du Soleil
at the Auberge du Soleil

Few places evoke the Mediterranean character of California's wine country as thoroughly as the Auberge du Soleil ("inn of the sun"), a luxurious country estate in a 33-acre olive grove on the eastern reaches of the Napa Valley. Its 50 suites, housed in earth-toned cottages overlooking the vines, are clearly meant for romance: French windows open to expansive terraces, fireplaces are stocked daily with wood, oversized tubs are set under skylights, and king-size beds are made with Frette linens. Winding paths, a sculpture garden, and three striking outdoor pools add to its appeal. The 7,000-square-foot spa is designed around a courtyard with stone fountains and 100-year-old olive trees, giving it the feel of a medieval abbey. Each of the six treatment rooms opens to a private patio with outdoor tub or shower. The spa menu reflects the bounty of fresh local ingredients, organizing its offerings into four different categories. Valley treatments are based on mud and minerals; Grove treatments make use of olive oil; Garden treatments utilize herbs and flowers; and Vineyard treatments take their cue from grapes. For the ultimate indulgence, book the four-hour Opus, which uses antioxidant-rich grape seeds in a series of treatments including herbal steam, exfoliation, a body mask, and a facial.

SIGNATURE TREATMENT: OPUS, FRESH HERBAL TEA AND STEAM THERAPY

Nur wenige Hotels fangen den mediterranen Charakter von Kaliforniens Weinregion so gut ein wie die Auberge du Soleil. Der luxuriöse Landsitz liegt in einem 13 Hektar großen Olivenhain im Osten des Napa Valley. Die 50 Suiten sind auf terrakottafarbene Cottages mit Blick auf die Rebstöcke verteilt und bieten genau das Richtige für frisch Verliebte: Fenstertüren gehen auf großzügige Terrassen hinaus, in die Kamine wird täglich neues Brennholz nachgelegt, unter den Dachfenstern stehen riesige Badewannen und die großen Doppelbetten sind mit Frette-Bettwäsche bezogen. Gewundene Wege, ein Skulpturenpark sowie drei prächtige Außenpools tragen ebenfalls zum Reiz dieser Anlage bei. Das 650 Quadratmeter große Spa umschließt einen Innenhof mit Steinbrunnen und hundertjährigen Olivenbäumen. Bei seinem Anblick fühlt man sich in ein mittelalterliches Kloster versetzt. Jeder der sechs Behandlungsräume geht auf einen eigenen Patio mit Außenbecken oder Dusche hinaus. Das auf frischen, lokalen Zutaten basierende Spa-Angebot ist in vier unterschiedliche Kategorien unterteilt. Die „Valley Treatments" basieren auf Schlamm und Mineralien, „Grove Treatments" verwenden Olivenöl, „Garden Treatments" nutzen die Wirkung von Kräutern und Blumen, während das „Vineyard Treatment" auf Trauben basiert. Den ultimativen Luxus jedoch liefert die vierstündige „Opus"-Anwendung. Auch sie nutzt die für ihre Antioxidantien berühmte Traube für Behandlungen wie Kräuterdampf, Peeling, Ganzkörper- und Gesichtsmaske.

WELLNESS-SPECIAL: OPUS

Peu d'endroits évoquent le caractère méditerranéen des régions vinicoles de Californie comme l'Auberge du Soleil, luxueux manoir situé en plein cœur d'une oliveraie de 13 hectares dominant la Napa Valley. Ses 50 suites, abritées dans des villas ocre donnant sur les vignes, invitent à la romance : les portes-fenêtres ouvrent sur de vastes terrasses, les cheminées sont approvisionnées en bois quotidiennement, les grandes baignoires sont placées sous les lucarnes et les immenses lits sont faits avec du linge Frette. Des sentiers sinueux, un jardin orné de sculptures et trois belles piscines extérieures ajoutent au charme du domaine. D'une superficie de 650 mètres carrés, le spa s'organise autour d'une cour intérieure ornée de fontaines en pierre et d'oliviers centenaires, conférant à l'ensemble l'aspect d'une abbaye médiévale. Chacune des six salles de soins donne sur un patio privatif équipé d'une baignoire ou d'une douche extérieure. Reflétant l'abondance et la fraîcheur des ingrédients locaux, les soins sont classés en quatre catégories. Les soins de la Vallée sont à base de boue et de minéraux ; les soins de l'Oliveraie exploitent les vertus de l'huile d'olive ; les soins du Jardin sont élaborés à partir de plantes et de fleurs, et les soins de la Vigne tirent parti des propriétés du raisin. Pour le plaisir suprême, il ne faut pas manquer l'Opus, d'une durée de quatre heures, à base de pépins de raisin riches en antioxydants utilisés dans une série de soins comprenant un bain de vapeur aromatique, une exfoliation, un masque corporel et un masque pour le visage.

SOIN PHARE : OPUS

Spa du Soleil at the Auberge du Soleil
180 Rutherford Hill Road
Rutherford, CA 94573
United States

TEL: +1 707 9631211
FAX: +1 707 9638764
EMAIL: info@aubergedusoleil.com
WEBSITE: www.aubergedusoleil.com

Tru

Tru is an ethereal space that offers a tranquil escape from city life in the heart of downtown San Francisco. Designed by architect Chris Kofitsas, the spa's clean lines, airy spaces, and use of light provide a modern minimalist environment. Tru offers massage, nail services, wet treatments, waxing, facials, and body treatments. It also boasts a one-of-a-kind rainforest room, which provides the setting for TRU's signature body treatments. Within the Amazon-evoking enclave, one can experience a distinct body wrap/steam while mellow jungle music plays in the background to really get you in the mood. Another custom feature is the spa's computer-controlled "colorblast" light therapy utilized during mood-enhancing massage experiences. Each room has different lighting depending on the type of massage one receives. Tru's modern design plays a significant role in the simple and straightforward design and concept of the spa. In the spa's reception and retail spaces, cool shades of blue and white, natural bamboo floors, and glowing Plexiglas panels create a feeling of floating and luminosity, while curving walls and conical fabric sculptures leading to the treatment rooms create a rhythm to the spa's rectangular space. The treatments focus primarily on effectiveness through exfoliation, extractions, and massage.

SIGNATURE TREATMENT: TRU 02 OXYGEN FACIAL

Das Tru ist eine Oase, in der man sich vom hektischen Treiben in der Altstadt von San Francisco erholen kann. Entworfen wurde sie von dem Architekten Chris Kofitsas, dem mit seinen klarlinigen, luft- und lichtdurchfluteten Räumen ein zeitgemäßes, minimalistisches Ambiente gelang. Im Tru werden Massagen, Maniküre, Nassbehandlungen, Haarentfernung, Gesichts- und Ganzkörperbehandlungen angeboten. Berühmt ist das Spa für seinen einzigartigen Regenwald-Raum, in dem das Wellness-Special durchgeführt wird. In einer an den amazonischen Regenwald erinnernden Atmosphäre erhält man eine Dampfbehandlung inklusive Bodywrap, während im Hintergrund fröhliche Dschungelmusik für die richtige Stimmung sorgt. Eine weitere Besonderheit des Spa ist seine computergesteuerte Lichttherapie, die für ganz besondere Massage-Erlebnisse sorgt: Je nachdem, für welche Massage man sich entscheidet, wird der Raum unterschiedlich beleuchtet. Das moderne Design des TRU Spa ist fester Bestandteil des Konzepts: Im Rezeptions- und Verkaufsbereich herrschen kühle Blau- und Weißtöne vor. Natürliche Bodenbeläge aus Bambus und leuchtende Plexiglaswände sorgen für viel Licht und Leichtigkeit. Auf dem Weg zu den Behandlungsräumen bilden gewellte Wände und kegelförmige Skulpturen ein harmonisches Gegengewicht zum rechteckigen Grundriss. Was die Behandlungen betrifft, ist das Spa auf Peelings, Tiefenreinigung und Massagen spezialisiert.

WELLNESS-SPECIAL: TRU 02 OXYGEN-GESICHTSBEHANDLUNG

Le TRU est un espace éthéré qui permet de s'évader de la vie citadine en plein cœur de San Francisco. Conçu par l'architecte Chris Kofitsas, ce spa offre des lignes pures et des espaces aériens tandis que l'utilisation de la lumière crée un environnement moderne et minimaliste. L'établissement propose des massages, des séances de manucure, des soins humides, des soins à la cire, des masques et des soins corporels. Il dispose également d'une salle unique en son genre, véritable forêt tropicale dans laquelle sont prodigués les meilleurs soins. Dans cette enclave évoquant l'Amazonie, bains de vapeur et enveloppements sont pratiqués au son d'une agréable musique d'ambiance reproduisant les sons de la forêt tropicale. Autre spécialité de l'établissement : la luminothérapie (grâce à un système de diodes électroluminescentes commandées par ordinateur) utilisée lors de séances de massage destinées à favoriser l'équilibre psychique. Chaque salle dispose d'un éclairage différent qui dépend du type de massage. La modernité du design joue un rôle prépondérant dans la conception sobre et pure du spa. Dans les espaces privatifs et de réception, les tons frais de bleu et de blanc, les sols en bambou naturel et les panneaux en plexiglas brillants créent une sensation de légèreté et de luminosité, tandis que les murs incurvés et les sculptures coniques en tissu conduisant aux salles de soins donnent un certain rythme aux lignes rectangulaires du spa. Les soins se veulent avant tout efficaces et privilégient les exfoliations, les extractions et les massages.

SOIN PHARE : SOIN DU VISAGE OXYGÈNE TRU 02

Tru
750 Kearny Street
San Francisco, CA 94108
United States

TEL: +1 415 3999700
FAX: no fax available
EMAIL: info@truspa.com
WEBSITE: www.truspa.com

The Kenwood Inn & Spa

Picture the rolling hills of Tuscany and the ambience of a rambling Mediterranean villa. Although it's just off Sonoma Valley's main highway, the Kenwood Inn is the sensory equivalent of a European countryside retreat, overlooking 2,000 acres of some of the most beautiful vineyards in the region. The central hub of the 30-suite property is a verdant courtyard with an oversized pool, surrounded by cushioned lounge chairs and shaded by ivy-covered trellises. A fully stocked wet bar is available in the adjoining lounge. The nearby millhouse encloses waterfalls and a steam room; another courtyard features a mineral Jacuzzi pool. Rooms are lavish and tasteful, with sprawling feather beds, ultramodern stereos, and a well-edited collection of CDs. (The absence of TVs makes for a hushed, romantic atmosphere.) The Caudalie Vinothérapie Spa, first of its kind in the U.S., is the sister property of the acclaimed original Caudalie spa in Bordeaux, France. Products draw from natural vine and grape extracts, known for their remarkable ability to trap free radicals and benefit the skin. The Caudalie Grand Facial Treatment is a cult classic; performed entirely by hand, it uses specific massage techniques in conjunction with the products to stimulate cell renewal and improve skin texture.

SIGNATURE TREATMENT: CAUDALIE GRANDE FACIAL TREATMENT

Denken Sie an die Hügellandschaft der Toskana und eine weitläufige Villa im mediterranen Stil: Obwohl sich das Kenwood Inn mitten im kalifornischen Sonoma Valley befindet, erinnert es eher an einen europäischen Landsitz. Von hier aus hat man einen fantastischen Blick auf rund 800 Hektar der schönsten Weinberge der Region. In der Mitte der Anlage mit 30 Suiten liegt ein begrünter Innenhof mit einem riesigen Pool, der von gepolsterten Liegestühlen gesäumt wird. Efeuumrankte Spaliere spenden angenehmen Schatten. Zu der angrenzenden Lounge gehört eine gut sortierte Wet-Bar. In der nahe gelegenen Mühle sind Wasserfallbecken und ein Dampfraum untergebracht. Ein weiterer Innenhof verfügt über einen mit Mineralien angereicherten Jacuzzi-Pool. Die Zimmer sind ebenso elegant wie geschmackvoll eingerichtet mit breiten Federbetten, ultramodernen Stereoanlagen und einer sorgfältig zusammengestellten CD-Sammlung. (Auf Fernseher wurde bewusst verzichtet, um die romantische Atmosphäre nicht zu stören.) Das Caudalie-Vinotherapie-Spa – übrigens das erste in den USA – ist ein Ableger des berühmten Caudalie-Spa im Bordeaux. Die Produkte basieren auf naturbelassenen Wein- und Traubenextrakten, die nachweislich Freie Radikale unschädlich machen und der Haut gut tun. Die Große Caudalie-Gesichtsbehandlung ist bereits zum Kult avanciert: Dabei werden die Produkte mit einer ganz besonderen Technik von Hand einmassiert, um die Zellerneuerung anzuregen und die Hautstruktur zu verbessern.

WELLNESS-SPECIAL: CAUDALIE-GESICHTSBEHANDLUNG

On se croirait dans les collines de Toscane et l'ambiance rappelle celle d'une villa méditerranéenne aux multiples recoins. Et pourtant, The Kenwood Inn se trouve à deux pas de la route principale desservant la Sonoma Valley. Cet établissement aux allures de maison de campagne européenne domine quelque 800 hectares de vignes parmi les plus belles de la région. Ses 30 suites s'organisent autour d'un patio verdoyant avec piscine et bains de soleil, à l'ombre de treillis recouverts de lierre. Un vaste bar est à la disposition des hôtes dans le salon voisin. Le moulin abrite des cascades et une étuve. Dans une autre cour se trouve un jacuzzi d'eau minérale. Dans les chambres, paisibles et raffinées, les couettes sont moelleuses, les chaînes stéréo ultramodernes et les CD bien choisis. (L'absence de téléviseurs favorise une atmosphère calme et romantique.) Unique aux États-Unis, le Caudalie Vinotherapie Spa est une réplique du spa de vinothérapie de Bordeaux. Les produits utilisés sont élaborés à base de vin et d'extraits naturels de raisin dont les propriétés sont bien connues pour combattre les radicaux libres et rajeunir la peau. Le masque intégral Caudalie est un grand classique. Entièrement réalisé à la main, ce soin recourt à des techniques de massage associées à des produits destinés à stimuler le renouvellement des cellules et à améliorer la texture de la peau.

SOIN PHARE: MASQUE INTÉGRAL CAUDALIE

The Kenwood Inn & Spa
10400 Sonoma Highway
Kenwood, CA 95452
United States

TEL: +1 707 8331293
FAX: +1 707 8331247
EMAIL: reservations@kenwoodinn.com
WEBSITE: www.kenwoodinn.com

International Orange

International Orange offers a sophisticated yet relaxed environment for both yoga practice and spa treatments. The white- and dark-wood minimalist interior features a light-filled yoga studio that evokes more a modern art gallery than the 60s ashram vibe of so many other yoga centers. Accordingly, International Orange presents a rotating program of installations by contemporary painters and sculptors throughout the space. This is only one of the small details that makes this city day-spa unique – other touches, include the candlelight and bowl of floating orchid blossoms in the impeccably maintained treatment rooms; an elegant tableaux of truffles, cheese and fruit in the lounge; and the unique terry robes designed by one of the spa's owners. The intimate lounge/waiting area features furniture inspired by minimalist sculptor Donald Judd, softened by fur throws and those decadent robes that you envelop yourself in before going in for treatments. International Orange's Spa and Yoga services are restorative remedies designed to encourage the body's natural healing capabilities. The spa utilizes plant-based products enriched with organic herbal extracts, essential oils, and fresh ingredients. After Ashtanga or IO's signature Scrub with Honey Glaze, the beautifully landscaped deck out back is a great place to continue to unwind.

SIGNATURE TREATMENT: SCRUB WITH HONEY GLAZE

Das International Orange bietet ein ebenso elegantes wie lässiges Ambiente. Die minimalistische Inneneinrichtung erstreckt sich auch auf das Yoga-Studio, das eher an eine moderne Kunstgalerie erinnert als an die ashramähnlichen Ausstattungen der 1960er Jahre. Da ist es nur konsequent, dass das International Orange in seinen Räumen Wechselausstellungen von zeitgenössischen Malern und Bildhauern zeigt. Dies ist jedoch nur ein Detail neben anderen, die dieses Day-Spa so besonders machen. In den makellos gepflegten Behandlungsräumen sorgen brennende Kerzen sowie Schalen mit Orchideenblüten für das gewisse Extra, während die Lounge Trüffelpralinen, Käse, Obst und einzigartige, von einem der Besitzer selbst entworfene Frotteebademäntel bereit hält. Der Wartebereich ist mit Möbeln eingerichtet, die an die Skulpturen des minimalistischen Künstlers Donald Judd erinnern. Fellüberwürfe und die bereits erwähnten Bademäntel sorgen für Gemütlichkeit. Das Spa- und Yoga-Angebot von International Orange will die Selbstheilungskräfte des Körpers auf natürliche Weise aktivieren. Daher verwendet das Spa ausschließlich Produkte auf Pflanzenbasis, die mit Biokräuterextrakten, essenziellen Ölen und frischen Zutaten angereichert sind. Nach der Ashtanga-Anwendung oder dem Wellness-Special, einem Salz-Honig-Peeling, kann man sich auf der Dachterrasse weiter entspannen.

WELLNESS-SPECIAL: SALZ-HONIG-PEELING

L'International Orange offre un cadre à la fois sophistiqué et apaisant pour prendre soin de son corps et pratiquer le yoga. L'intérieur minimaliste tout de blanc et de noir abrite une salle de yoga qui évoque davantage une galerie d'art moderne qu'un ashram des années 1960 empli de vibrations spirituelles. L'International Orange accueille d'ailleurs régulièrement des expositions de peintres et de sculpteurs contemporains. Mais ce n'est là qu'une facette de cet exceptionnel spa de jour. Il se distingue également par de nombreux détails comme les bougies et les coupes d'orchidées flottantes dans les salles de soins impeccablement entretenues, un superbe assortiment de truffes, de fromages et de fruits dans le salon ou les peignoirs créés spécialement par l'un des propriétaires de l'établissement. Le confortable salon/salle d'attente est décoré de meubles inspirés du sculpteur minimaliste Donald Judd, et l'ambiance est adoucie par les couvertures de fourrure et ces luxueux peignoirs dans lesquels on aime à s'envelopper avant de se rendre dans les salles de soins. Les séances de yoga et les soins proposés par l'International Orange ont pour but de favoriser le potentiel régénérateur naturel du corps. À base de plantes, les produits utilisés sont enrichis en extraits végétaux organiques, en huiles essentielles et en ingrédients frais. Après une séance d'ashtanga yoga ou un gommage au miel, rien de tel qu'une pause en terrasse pour admirer le magnifique paysage et prolonger ces moments de détente.

SOIN PHARE: GOMMAGE AU MIEL

International Orange
2044 Fillmore Street
San Francisco, CA 94115
United States

TEL: +1 415 5635000
FAX: +1 415 5635500
EMAIL: info@internatinalorange.com
WEBSITE: www.internationalorange.com

Agua at the Delano Hotel

Located in the center of South Beach, directly on the ocean, the Delano is a surrealist urban resort. With little separation between indoors and out in the hotel's public spaces, the hotel projects a relaxed, though very stylish, attitude. Ideal for people-watching, Delano's indoor/outdoor lobby was inspired by the sidewalk cafés in Venice's San Marco square and the "hotel as theater" concept. The hotel has 238 rooms, suites, lofts, apartments, and bungalows, including some adjacent to the distinctive quartz swimming pool and water salon. Typical of its designer, Philippe Starck, Delano's decor is dramatic and chic, characterized by white wooden floors, mirrored walls, marble accents, and open doors with breezy curtains. The chic lounge features a custom-built 15-foot-long bar and a 12-foot paneled screen fashioned out of hand-etched Venetian mirrors. Agua, the rooftop women's bathhouse and solarium, offers massages, facials, aromatherapy body treatments, and meditation developed by former New York City ballet dancer Rita Norona Schrager. Recalling the ancient Roman Baths, the spa's dreamy water salon has spaces for floating, meditating, or sleeping. The hotel also features a sunroof and conservatory, state-of-the-art gymnasium, indoor/outdoor fitness areas, and fitness classes on the beach. In-room massage and spa treatments are also available.

SIGNATURE TREATMENT: MILK & HONEY

Das im Herzen von South Beach gelegene Delano befindet sich direkt am Meer und zugleich mitten in der Großstadt. In dem unaufdringlichen Design-Hotel gehen Drinnen und Draußen nahtlos ineinander über. So erinnert die Indoor-/Outdoor-Lobby des Delano an die Arkadencafés auf dem Markusplatz in Venedig. Hier sitzt man wie auf einer Bühne und kann die Passanten beobachten. Die Hotelanlage besteht aus 238 Zimmern, Suiten, Lofts, Apartments und Bungalows. Einige davon liegen direkt am durchgestylten Quartz-Swimming-Pool mit Wasser-Salon. Wie vom Designer Philippe Starck nicht anders zu erwarten, ist die Innenausstattung ebenso originell wie edel: Weiße Holzdielen, verspiegelte Wände, Marmorakzente und offene Durchgänge mit luftigen Gardinen. Das Agua, ein auf der Dachterrasse gelegenes Badehaus mit Solarium für Frauen, bietet Massagen, Gesichtsbehandlungen, Aromatherapie-Körperbehandlungen sowie Meditationskurse an, die von der ehemaligen Tänzerin des New York City Ballet, Norona Schrager, entwickelt wurden. Der traumhaft schöne Wasser-Salon des Spa lässt die altrömische Badekultur wieder aufleben. Hier kann man sich treiben lassen, meditieren oder einfach vor sich hindösen. Des weiteren verfügt das Hotel über Sonnendeck, Wintergarten, ein perfekt ausgestattetes Fitness-Studio und Indoor-/Outdoor-Fitnessbereiche. Direkt am Strand werden ebenfalls Fitnesskurse angeboten. Und wer möchte, kann sich auch auf dem Hotelzimmer mit Massagen und Spa-Behandlungen verwöhnen lassen.

WELLNESS-SPECIAL: MILCH & HONIG

Situé en plein centre de South Beach et donnant directement sur l'océan, le Delano est un complexe urbain surréaliste alliant détente et élégance. Idéale pour regarder passer les gens, l'entrée du Delano s'inspire des terrasses de la place Saint-Marc à Venise et du concept de l'« hôtel-théâtre ». L'hôtel compte 238 chambres, suites, lofts, appartements et bungalows, dont certains sont situés à proximité de la belle piscine en quartz et du spa. Signée Philippe Starck, la décoration est impressionnante et raffinée, avec des sols blancs en bois, des murs recouverts de miroirs, quelques touches de marbre et des ouvertures aux rideaux qui ondulent sous la brise. Le grand salon dispose d'un bar long de 4,5 mètres, construit sur mesure, et d'un paravent de 3,5 mètres fabriqué à partir de miroirs vénitiens gravés à la main. Sur les toits, le centre Agua (bains et solarium pour femmes) propose des massages, des masques, des soins aromatiques et des séances de méditation mises au point par l'ex-danseuse classique new-yorkaise Rita Norona Schrager. Rappelant les thermes romains, le spa et ses différents espaces réservés à la baignade, à la méditation et au repos font rêver. L'hôtel dispose également d'une terrasse, d'une serre, d'un gymnase ultramoderne, de salles de fitness intérieures et extérieures. Massages et soins corporels sont également disponibles dans les chambres.

SOIN PHARE : LAIT & MIEL

Agua at the Delano Hotel
1685 Collins Avenue
Miami Beach, FL 33139
United States

TEL: +1 305 6722000
FAX: +1 305 5320099
EMAIL: delanoreservation@morganshotelgroup.com
WEBSITE: www.morganshotelgroup.com

Château Élan Spa

Romance is a key ingredient in the approach at the Château Élan Spa, where the ambience and treatments have been created in the spirit of l'amour and are best appreciated à deux. Set within an imposing, French-style château overlooking a shimmering lake and surrounded by Arcadian lawns, lush vineyards, and sun-dappled forests, the residential spa seems closer to Europe than to Atlanta. Yet the state capital is but a 30-minute drive away. Individually themed guest rooms draw inspiration from across continents and eras. The Victorian Wicker Room, for example, features art and antiques from that age of decorous romance while the Zimbabwe Room's wildlife prints and carved creatures are straight out of Africa. And that's only the beginning. There's a setting to suit nearly every style or fantasy, with most of the 277 rooms featuring either a double-headed shower or a Jacuzzi made for two. These built-for-romance environments set the stage for the spa's signature treatment, an in-room couples massage lit with candlelight and scented with freshly strewn rose petals. This ultimate indulgence might mark the end of a day spent receiving a facial, body wrap, and more in the treatment room or simply strolling hand in hand along the spa's forested nature trail.

SIGNATURE TREATMENT: COUPLES MASSAGE

Im Château Élan Spa dreht sich alles um die Liebe: Einrichtung und Behandlungen sorgen für romantische Stimmung und sollten idealerweise zu zweit genossen werden. Untergebracht ist das Spa in einem imposanten, französisch anmutendem Château mit Blick auf einen funkelnden See, idyllische Wiesen, üppige Weinberge und sonnengesprenkelte Wälder. Von hier aus scheint man schneller in Europa zu sein als in Atlanta. Und trotzdem braucht man bis zur Hauptstadt des gleichnamigen Bundesstaats gerade einmal 30 Minuten mit dem Auto. Die von verschiedenen Kontinenten und Epochen inspirierten Gästezimmer wurden alle nach einem anderen Motto gestaltet. Das viktorianische Korbmöbelzimmer schmücken Kunst und Antiquitäten, während die Raubtierdrucke und Holzskulpturen im Zimbabwe-Zimmer direkt aus Afrika stammen. Aber das ist erst der Anfang: Hier gibt es für jeden Geschmack das passende Ambiente. Die meisten der 277 Zimmer haben Duschen mit zwei Duschköpfen oder einen Jacuzzi, in dem man auch zu zweit Platz findet. Romantisch wird es auch beim Wellness-Special des Spa: Die eigens für Paare entwickelte Massage findet in einem mit duftenden Rosenblättern ausgelegten Behandlungsraum bei Kerzenlicht statt. Dieses ultimative Verwöhnprogramm ist der ideale Abschluss eines Schönheitstags mit Gesichtsbehandlungen, Bodywraps und anderen Anwendungen. Aber auch nach einem romantischen Waldspaziergang auf dem Spa-eigenen Naturlehrpfad ist so eine Massage durchaus zu empfehlen.

WELLNESS-SPECIAL: MASSAGE FÜR PAARE

Le Château Élan Spa est placé sous le signe de l'amour et tous les soins qui y sont prodigués peuvent s'apprécier à deux. Installé dans un imposant château de style français construit au bord d'un lac et entouré de vastes pelouses, de vignes abondantes et de bois taquinés par le soleil, ce spa rappelle davantage l'Europe qu'Atlanta, qui n'est pourtant qu'à une demi-heure en voiture. Les chambres à thèmes s'inspirent de tous les continents et de toutes les époques. Ainsi, la chambre Victorienne en osier est décorée d'œuvres et d'objets d'art datant de cette époque de charmante bienséance, tandis que la chambre Zimbabwe, avec ses gravures florales et animalières et ses créatures sculptées, vient tout droit d'Afrique. Mais ce ne sont que deux exemples. Chacun peut en effet trouver la chambre qui correspond à son style ou à son idée, la plupart des 277 chambres étant équipées d'une douche double ou d'un jacuzzi pour deux. Un tel cadre romantique invite naturellement à découvrir la spécialité de l'établissement: un massage pour deux, en chambre, aux chandelles et parfumé aux pétales de rose délicatement clairsemés. Ce plaisir suprême peut couronner la fin d'une journée passée à profiter des masques, enveloppements et autres soins proposés par le spa, ou simplement à se promener main dans la main sur les sentiers forestiers du domaine.

SOIN PHARE: MASSAGES POUR COUPLES

Château Élan Spa
100 Rue Charlemagne
Braselton, GA 30517
United States

TEL: +1 678 4250900
FAX: +1 678 4256000
EMAIL: chateau@chateauelan.com
WEBSITE: www.chateauelan.com

The Kahala
Hotel & Resort

Ten minutes from Waikiki, in the prestigious residential neighborhood of Kahala, the Kahala Hotel & Resort rests on a secluded crescent-shaped beach overlooking Diamond Head and Koko Head craters. Originally built in 1964 by Conrad Hilton (and featured in episodes of *Magnum, P. I.* and *Hawaii Five-O*), the resort has the feel of a grand Hawaiian plantation home. Turn-of-the-twentieth-century Hawaiian furnishings fill the 364 rooms, along with teak parquet floors, hand-loomed Tibetan rugs and distinctive works by local artists. A natural saltwater lagoon is home to five well-loved Atlantic bottlenose dolphins. A lounge sheltered by stalks of giant bamboo welcomes guests to the Spa Suites; each named after a different Hawaiian flower, the 550-square-foot suites comprise a changing area, private shower, relaxation lounge, infinity-edge soaking bath, and garden. Polished mahogany, rattan cushions, and floating candles provide a tranquil backdrop; massage beds are draped with traditional Hawaiian quilts, hand-stitched by hotel staff. Almost all treatments begin with a ritual foot cleansing in aromatic water blended with Hawaiian sea salts. The two-and-a-half-hour Lokahi experience starts with an aromatic bath, body brushing, and exfoliating body polish with aloe, followed by a massage with kukui and macadamia nut oils.

SIGNATURE TREATMENT: LOKAHI

Zehn Minuten von Waikiki entfernt, unweit des Nobelviertels Kahala, liegt an einem einsamen, sichelförmigen Strand das Kahala Hotel & Resort. Von hier aus hat man einen herrlichen Blick auf die Krater des Diamond und des Koko Head. Das 1964 von Conrad Hilton errichtete Hotel, in dem Episoden von *Magnum* und *Hawaii Fünf-Null* gedreht wurden, wirkt wie das große Herrenhaus eines Plantagenbesitzers. Hawaiische Möbel vom Beginn des 20. Jahrhunderts zieren die 364 Zimmer, die mit Teakholzparkett, handgewebten Tibet-Teppichen und unverwechselbaren Arbeiten einheimischer Künstler ausgestattet sind. In der natürlichen Salzwasserlagune leben fünf heißgeliebte Atlantische Tümmler. Jede der etwa 50 Quadratmeter großen Spa-Suiten umfasst Umkleideraum, eigene Dusche, Lounge, Naturpool sowie einen kleinen Garten. Poliertes Mahagoni, Rattan, Kissen und Schwimmkerzen sorgen für ein angenehmes Ambiente. Die Massageliegen schmücken traditionelle hawaiische Quilts, die von Hotelangestellten handbestickt wurden. Fast alle Behandlungen beginnen mit einem Fußreinigungsritual, für das parfümiertes Wasser mit hawaiischen Meersalzen verwendet wird. Die zweieinhalbstündige Lokahi-Anwendung dagegen beginnt mit einem duftenden Bad, gefolgt von einer Ganzkörperbürstenmassage sowie einem Peeling mit Aloe Vera. Den Abschluss bildet eine Massage mit Kukui- und Makadamianussölen.

WELLNESS-SPECIAL: LOKAHI

À dix minutes de Waikiki, dans les prestigieux environs résidentiels de Kahala, le Kahala Hotel & Resort s'étend sur une plage discrète en forme de croissant donnant sur les cratères du Diamond Head et du Koko Head. Construit en 1964 par Conrad Hilton, l'établissement (qui a notamment servi de lieu de tournage pour *Magnum*) évoque une grande maison de planteur. Les 364 chambres sont décorées de meubles hawaïens datant du début du XXe siècle, mais également de parquets en teck, de tapis tibétains tissés à la main et d'œuvres caractéristiques d'artistes locaux. Un lagon naturel d'eau salée est le refuge de cinq adorables dauphins à gros nez de l'Atlantique. À l'abri de grandes pousses de bambou, un salon accueille les hôtes du Spa Suites. Chaque suite – d'une cinquantaine de mètres carrés – porte le nom d'une fleur hawaïenne et dispose d'un vestiaire, d'une douche privée, d'une salle de relaxation, d'une grande baignoire et d'un jardin. Acajou poli, meubles en rotin et bougies flottantes agrémentent ce cadre d'une douce sérénité. Les tables de massage sont recouvertes de courtepointes traditionnelles cousues à la main par le personnel de l'hôtel. La plupart des soins commencent par une purification rituelle des pieds dans de l'eau aromatisée mélangée à des sels de mer hawaïens. D'une durée de deux heures et demie, le soin Lokahi commence par un bain aromatique, se poursuit par un gommage corporel et une exfoliation à l'aloès, et s'achève par un massage aux huiles de kukui et de noix de macadamia.

SOIN PHARE: LOKAHI

The Kahala Hotel & Resort

5000 Kahala Avenue

Honolulu, HI 96816

United States

TEL: +1 808 739 8888

FAX: +1 808 739 8800

EMAIL: kahala-reservations@kahalaresort.com

WEBSITE: www.kahalaresort.com

Spa Halekulani

Honolulu, Hawaii

In Hawaiian, "halekulani" means "house befitting heaven." The 455-room hotel and spa given this name aim to live up to it. Within the resort's five secluded acres of otherwise overcrowded Waikiki beach, spa master Sylvia Sepielli has created an intimate refuge showcasing the decorative arts and healing traditions of the Pacific islands. The open-plan reception area features a trickling fountain, citrus-colored walls, and glistening bamboo floors. Original prints of tropical blossoms line the corridor leading to the treatment rooms, venues for the spa's specialty: the four-hour Heavenly Journey. Guests plan their itinerary from a list of indigenous massage and facial techniques. Lomi Lomi is one such option, a massage technique based on the ancient teachings of Hawaiian kahuna, the island version of medicine men. To improve energy flow and thus release built-up tension, the masseuse uses long, fluid strokes, her hands and forearms lubricated with aromatic oils. Gentle rotation of the joints and moderate stretching further invigorate the body; the practitioner's round-the-table hula energizes the environs and the spirit. A luxurious, vitamin-rich facial using potions made from tropical plants might be the next stop, before drifting out toward the swaying palms and relaxing to the rhythmic sounds of the surf on the spa's beachfront terrace.

SIGNATURE TREATMENT: HEAVENLY JOURNEY

„Halekulani" ist hawaiisch und bedeutet „paradiesisches Haus" – ein Name, dem das 455-Betten-Hotel und Spa mehr als gerecht wird. Innerhalb der ruhigen, etwas über zwei Hektar großen Anlage hat die Spa-Chefin Sylvia Sepielli am überlaufenen Waikiki-Beach eine echte Oase geschaffen. Hier hat man sich ganz der Kunst und den Heiltraditionen der Pazifikinseln verschrieben. Der durchgehende Rezeptionsbereich besticht durch einen plätschernden Brunnen, zitronengelbe Wände und glänzendes Bambus-Parkett. Das Wellness-Special ist eine vierstündige Anwendung namens „Heavenly Journey". Diese Reise kann sich der Gast aus einheimischen Massagetechniken und Gesichtsbehandlungen selbst zusammenstellen. Lomi Lomi ist eine mögliche Station: Diese Massagetechnik beruht auf den alten Lehren der hawaiianischen „kahuna", der Medizinmänner der Insel. Um den Energiefluss zu verbessern und Verspannungen zu lösen, führt die Masseurin lange, fließende Streichbewegungen aus. Ihre Hände und Unterarme sind mit aromatischen Ölen eingesalbt. Sanfte Dreh- und Dehnbewegungen erwecken den Körper zu neuem Leben. Der um den Massagetisch absolvierte Hula-Tanz der Therapeutin belebt die Atmosphäre und den Geist. Eine vitaminreiche Gesichtsmaske mit tropischen Pflanzensäften könnte das nächste Etappenziel sein, bevor auf der Spa-eigenen Terrasse der Brandung lauscht.

WELLNESS-SPECIAL: HEAVENLY JOURNEY

En hawaïen, « halekulani » signifie « maison paradisiaque ». L'hôtel avec 455 chambres et le spa du même nom ont donc pour seul but d'être à la hauteur de leur appellation. Sur un peu plus de deux hectares, à l'écart de la plage surpeuplée de Waikiki, la propriétaire du spa Sylvia Sepielli a créé un refuge discret inspiré des arts décoratifs et des techniques ancestrales de guérison des îles du Pacifique. Totalement ouvert, le hall de réception est orné d'une fontaine, de murs couleur citron et de sols brillants en bambou. Des gravures originales de fleurs tropicales jalonnent le couloir qui conduit aux salles de soins où se pratique la spécialité de l'établissement : le Voyage au paradis (quatre heures). Les hôtes tracent leur itinéraire en choisissant dans une liste de massages et de masques typiques du lieu. Le massage Lomi Lomi est une technique issue des enseignements des kahunas, guérisseurs de Hawaï. Afin de faire circuler l'énergie et de relâcher la tension, la masseuse, qui s'est enduit les mains et les avant-bras d'huiles aromatiques, avance par mouvements longs et continus. Une légère rotation des articulations et quelques étirements permettent de tonifier le corps davantage. Tandis que la masseuse exécute la danse du *hula* autour de la table, elle transmet son énergie à l'environnement et à l'esprit. Il ne reste plus qu'à se laisser tenter par un agréable masque riche en vitamines, élaboré à partir de plantes tropicales, avant de se diriger vers les palmiers qui se balancent au gré du vent et de se reposer sur la terrasse de l'établissement en se laissant bercer par le rythme des vagues.

SOIN PHARE : VOYAGE AU PARADIS

Spa Halekulani
2199 Kalia Road
Honolulu, HI 96815
United States

TEL: +1 808 9315322
FAX: +1 808 9315321
EMAIL: spa.halekulani@halekulani.com
WEBSITE: www.halekulani.com

Four Seasons Resort Hualalai at Historic Ka'upulehu

Hawaii's Kona-Kohala coast, where the Four Seasons Resort Hualalai with its 243 rooms and suites is located, is so stunning that it's hard to know where to look. Blacker-than-black lava rock, swaying palm trees, seemingly limitless sunshine, and an endless shimmering sea. It's no wonder that the concept of the renowned Hualalai Sports Club and Spa is to bring inside a taste of the outdoors. Nine outdoor massage hales (or huts), outdoor showers, open-air gyms, glass-walled outdoor steam and saunas, and a grass yoga/meditation courtyard combine to do just that. The club and spa provide guests with the perfect environment for their ideal combination of physical activity, mental relaxation, and body rejuvenation. The spa's massage treatments (performed in the relaxing treatment rooms or outside in the hale) range from the vigorous Hawaiian lomi lomi and Japanese shiatsu to Swedish, Thai, and reiki. The "Hone Huali" or South Seas Sugar Body Scrub is a decadent 50-minute signature treatment designed to hydrate and exfoliate the skin, and incorporates a blend of essential oils, Hawaiian cane sugar, coconut, and therapeutic lehua honey. Fitness options range from tennis to weight training to volleyball, not to mention the opportunity to score the ultimate hole in one: the 18-hole signature Jack Nicklaus course, surrounded by Kona-Kohala's dramatic shoreline, offers the first hole playing directly toward Hualalai volcano.

SIGNATURE TREATMENT: HONE HUALI (SOUTH SEAS SUGAR BODY SCRUB)

Hawaiis Kailua-Kona-Küste, an der das Four Seasons Hualalai mit seinen 243 Gästezimmern und Suiten liegt, ist so atemberaubend, dass man gar nicht weiß, wohin man zuerst schauen soll – auf das pechschwarze Lavagestein, die sich im Wind wiegenden Palmen oder das in der Sonne glitzernde Meer. Kein Wunder also, dass es zum Konzept des Hualalai Sports Club & Spa gehört, den Blick auf diese herrliche Kulisse so unverstellt wie möglich zu belassen. Dafür sorgen offene Massagehütten, Außenduschen, ein Fitness-Studio im Freien, Dampfraum und Sauna mit Glaswänden sowie ein mit Rasen bewachsener Innenhof für Yoga und Meditation. Club und Spa bieten den Gästen das ideale Ambiente, um Sport zu treiben, sich zu entspannen und verjüngen zu lassen. Die Massagen, die entweder in Behandlungsräumen oder draußen in den Hütten angeboten werden, reichen von der hawaiianischen Lomi-Lomi- über die japanische Shiatsu- bis hin zur Schwedischen, Thai- oder Reiki-Massage. Beim „Hone Huali" befreien essenzielle Öle, hawaiianischer Rohrzucker, Kokosnuss und der therapeutische Lehua-Honig die Haut von abgestorbenen Hautzellen und spenden Feuchtigkeit. Die Sportmöglichkeiten reichen von Tennis über Krafttraining bis hin zum Volleyball. Der 18-Loch-Golfplatz liegt unmittelbar an der eindrucksvollen Küstenlinie von Kailua-Kona. Beim Abschlag spielt man direkt auf den Hualalai-Vulkan zu.

WELLNESS-SPECIAL: HONE-HUALI (SÜDSEEZUCKER-BODYPEELING)

La côte hawaïenne à Kailua-Kona, où se trouve le Four Seasons Hualalai avec ses 243 chambres et suites, est tellement impressionnante qu'il est difficile de savoir où regarder. Roches volcaniques d'un noir profond, palmiers se balançant au gré du vent, horizons ensoleillés, mer scintillante à l'infini... Le célèbre Hualalai Sports Club & Spa ne peut que refléter la beauté du cadre dans lequel il est situé. Avec ses neuf huttes de massage extérieures, ses douches extérieures, ses salles de gymnastique en plein air, son étuve et ses saunas extérieurs aux murs de verre et sa cour intérieure gazonnée réservée à la méditation et aux séances de yoga, l'établissement offre à ses hôtes un environnement idéal pour la pratique d'activités physiques, la relaxation mentale et le rajeunissement du corps. Les massages (pratiqués dans les reposantes salles de soins ou à l'extérieur, dans les huttes) vont du vigoureux Lomi Lomi hawaïen au shiatsu japonais, en passant par les massages suédois, thaïs et le reiki. D'une durée de 50 minutes, le « Hone Huali » ou gommage corporel sucré des mers du Sud, a pour but d'hydrater et d'exfolier la peau. Il est réalisé grâce à un mélange d'huiles essentielles, de canne à sucre de Hawaï, de noix de coco et de miel. Le Four Seasons Hualalai propose par ailleurs plusieurs activités sportives : tennis, musculation, volley-ball, sans oublier le golf, avec un parcours de 18 trous conçu par Jack Nicklaus. Avec la magnifique côte de Kailua-Kona en toile de fond, le premier trou du parcours permet de jouer directement dans l'axe du volcan Hualalai.

SOIN PHARE : HONE HUALI (GOMMAGE CORPOREL SUCRÉ DES MERS DU SUD)

Four Seasons Resort Hualalai
at Historic Ka'upulehu
72–100 Ka'upulehu Drive, Kailua-Kona, HI 96740
United States

TEL: +1 808 3258000
FAX: +1 808 3258200
EMAIL: world.reservations@fourseasons.com
WEBSITE: www.fourseasons.com/hualalai

The Fairmont Orchid

The Big Island, Hawaii

Along the pristine Kohala Coast on the Big Island of Hawaii, hidden from the outside world by dramatic outcrops of lava rock, black as ebony, is the Fairmont Orchid. The 32-acre oceanfront resort features breathtaking views of the Pacific and the nearby Mauna Kea volcano. If you can tear yourself away from the view (and the Mai Tais), you can enjoy tennis, golf, fitness training, swimming, snorkeling, canoeing, and even a tour of a petroglyph preserve. But save time for the indulgence of the Spa Without Walls. As its name suggests, the spa maximizes Hawaii's natural environment with ancient healing arts by providing treatments that make the most of the property's beachfront locale. Body treatments are offered in secluded oceanfront cabanas, in a secluded teahouse adjacent to trickling waterfalls and lush tropical gardens, or in the privacy of one of the 540 guest rooms. Even yoga classes are available right by the sea. Within the walls of the spa, distinctive treatments are on offer, such as the signature Big Island Vanilla Coffee Exfoliation, which incorporates not only the Kona coffee for which the region is famous but also raw Hawaiian sugar, vanilla ("fruit of the orchid"), orange essential oil, kukui (candlenut oil), grapeseed oil, green tree extract, and ginseng.

SIGNATURE TREATMENT: BIG ISLAND VANILLA COFFEE EXFOLIATION

An der unberührten Kohala-Küste auf Big Island, Hawaii, liegt das durch bizarr geformtes, pechschwarzes Lavagestein abgeschirmte Fairmont Orchid. Von der zwölf Hektar großen Anlage hat man einen fantastischen Blick auf den Pazifik und den nahe gelegenen Mauna-Kea-Vulkan. Wer es schafft, sich von dieser atemberaubenden Kulisse (und den Mai Tais) loszureißen, kann Tennis spielen, golfen, im Fitness-Studio trainieren, schwimmen, schnorcheln, Kanu fahren, ja sogar alte Felszeichnungen besichtigen. Hauptsache, es bleibt noch genügend Zeit, sich im hoteleigenen „Spa ohne Wände" verwöhnen zu lassen. Hier kann man nicht nur alte Heiltraditionen, sondern auch die fantastische Naturkulisse genießen. Die Behandlungen erfolgen in einzelnen Cabanas mit Meerblick, in einem ruhig gelegenen Teehaus neben plätschernden Wasserfällen, in üppigen tropischen Gärten oder ganz privat auf einem der 540 Hotelzimmer. Sogar Yoga-Kurse werden direkt am Strand angeboten. Innerhalb des Spa-Areals wartet das hauseigene Wellness-Special, ein „Big Island" Vanille-Kaffee-Peeling. Dabei wird nicht nur mit Kona-Kaffee gearbeitet, für den die Gegend hier berühmt ist, sondern auch mit hawaiianischem Rohrzucker, Vanille (der „Frucht der Orchidee"), essenziellem Orangenöl, Kukuinussöl, Traubenkernöl, Grün-Tee-Extrakt und Ginseng.

WELLNESS-SPECIAL: VANILLE-KAFFEE-PEELING BIG ISLAND

Le long de la côte Kohala, sur la grande île de Hawaï, le Fairmont Orchid est dissimulé par de spectaculaires affleurements de roches volcaniques aussi noires que l'ébène. S'étendant sur une douzaine d'hectares, le domaine offre une vue imprenable sur l'océan Pacifique et sur le volcan Mauna Kea. Outre le magnifique panorama (et un délicieux cocktail Mai Tai), l'établissement propose de nombreuses activités : tennis, golf, fitness, natation, plongée en apnée, canoë et même une excursion-découverte des pétroglyphes de l'île. Sans oublier le Spa Without Walls ! Ce dernier tire le meilleur parti de l'environnement naturel de Hawaï et les soins s'inspirent de techniques ancestrales de guérison. Ils sont pratiqués dans des cabanes au bord de l'océan, dans une maison de thé à proximité de jolies cascades et de jardins tropicaux luxuriants, ou dans l'intimité d'une des 540 chambres de l'hôtel. Des séances de yoga ont également lieu en bord de mer. Le spa propose des soins variés, dont l'incontournable Exfoliation vanille-café de la grande île. Ce soin utilise non seulement le célèbre café Kona de Hawaï, mais également du sucre brut, de la vanille (« fruit de l'orchidée »), de l'huile essentielle d'orange, du kukui (huile de bancoulier), de l'huile de pépins de raisin, des extraits de thé vert et du ginseng.

SOIN PHARE : EXFOLIATION VANILLE-CAFÉ DE LA GRANDE ÎLE

The Fairmont Orchid
1 North Kaniku Drive
Kohala Coast, HI 96743
United States

TEL: +1 808 8852000
FAX: +1808 8855778
EMAIL: orchid@fairmont.com
WEBSITE: www.fairmont.com/orchid

259

Four Seasons Resort Maui at Wailea

The word "paradise" comes easily to mind at the Four Seasons Resort Maui at Wailea, a 15-acre spread of exotic gardens, fountains, pools, and lanais at the edge of the ocean offering 380 rooms and suites. The resort's philosophy is keenly tied to Hawaiian legend, which regards water as a symbol of rejuvenation and spirit. Accordingly, the Spa at the Four Seasons Resort Maui bases its own offerings on ancient Hawaiian traditions. The 21,000-square-foot facility has 13 new treatment rooms and a Healing Garden featuring more than 20 different types of native and medicinal plants and trees – from aloe vera to taro, kukui to coconut – that are incorporated into treatments and culinary menus. Three oceanside Hawaiian hales (thatched-roof huts) with views of Wailea Beach and the island of Lanai are available for massages. The new spa menu includes Hawaiian Temple Bodywork, which stems from a sacred healing ceremony and is performed in the oceanfront bamboo hut by at least two therapists working in unison, and the Ocean Cranio-Sacral Massage, which uses the rhythms of the sea to help release tension. There's even a couples suite, where guests can relax on heated cocoon beds before receiving a luxurious avocado and Hawaiian maile body mask.

SIGNATURE TREATMENT: HAWAIIAN TEMPLE BODYWORK

Im Four Seasons Resort Maui in Wailea – auf sechs Hektar mit exotischen Gärten, Brunnen, Pools und Veranden direkt am Meer – fühlt man sich wie im Paradies. Die Philosophie des Hotels, das 380 Zimmer und Suiten anbietet, ist eng mit einer hawaiischen Legende verknüpft, nach der das Element Wasser ein Symbol für Verjüngung und die Seele ist. Auch die Angebote des hauseigenen Spa beruhen auf alten hawaiischen Traditionen. Zu der 2.000 Quadratmeter großen Anlage gehören 13 neu errichtete Behandlungsräume und ein Garten, wo 20 verschiedene einheimische (Heil-)Pflanzen gedeihen – von Aloe Vera bis hin zu Taro, Kukuinussbaum und Kokospalme. Die Ernte von dort kommt nicht nur bei den Wellness-Behandlungen, sondern auch in der Küche zum Einsatz. Drei hawaiianische „Hales" (palmblattgedeckte Hütten) mit Blick auf den Wailea Beach und die Insel Lanai stehen für Massagen zur Verfügung. Zum neuen Spa-Angebot gehört die Hawaiische-Tempel-Anwendung, die von einer religiösen Heilzeremonie abgeleitet ist. Sie wird in einer Bambushütte direkt am Meer von zwei synchron arbeitenden Therapeuten ausgeführt. Oder man bucht die Ozean-Cranio-Sakral-Massage, bei der das Meeresrauschen für tiefe Entspannung sorgt. Speziell für Paare ist eine Suite eingerichtet, in der sich die Gäste auf beheizten Liegen ausruhen können, bevor sie eine üppige Körperpackung aus Avocado und hawaiianischen Maile-Blättern erhalten.

WELLNESS-SPECIAL: HAWAIISCHE TEMPEL-ANWENDUNG

C'est tout naturellement que le mot « paradis » vient à l'esprit pour décrire le Four Seasons Resort Maui, à Wailea, domaine de quelque six hectares avec jardins exotiques, fontaines, piscines et vérandas au bord de l'océan. La philosophie de l'établissement avec 380 chambres et suites est étroitement liée aux légendes hawaïennes relatives à l'eau, symbole de rajeunissement et d'esprit. Le spa du Four Seasons Resort Maui propose donc des soins qui s'inspirent des traditions ancestrales de Hawaï. Sur près de 2 000 mètres carrés s'étendent 13 nouvelles salles de soins et un jardin botanique abritant plus de 20 essences différentes d'arbres et de plantes médicinales indigènes (aloé vera, taro, kukui, noix de coco), à partir desquels les soins et les menus sont élaborés. Au bord de l'océan, trois huttes hawaïennes avec vue sur Wailea Beach et l'île de Lanai sont réservées aux massages. Dans une hutte en bambou donnant sur l'océan, le Massage du temple hawaïen, qui tire son origine d'un rituel sacré, est réalisé par deux thérapeutes au minimum qui travaillent de façon parfaitement synchronisée. Quant au Massage vertébral de l'océan, il recourt aux rythmes de la mer pour favoriser une détente complète du corps. L'établissement dispose même d'une suite pour deux où les hôtes peuvent se reposer sur des lits chauffés avant de savourer un masque corporel à l'avocat et au maile.

SOIN PHARE : MASSAGE DU TEMPLE HAWAÏEN

Four Seasons Resort Maui at Wailea
3900 Wailea Alanui
Wailea, HI 96753
United States

TEL: +1 808 8748000
FAX: +1 808 8742244
EMAIL: world.reservations@fourseasons.com
WEBSITE: www.fourseasons.com/maui

Ten Thousand Waves

Based on a traditional Japanese onsen (hot spring resort), Ten Thousand Waves has transported the East to the West. While staying true to its Asian roots, the spa incorporates a Southwest flair to highlight its Santa Fe surroundings. The minimalist architecture and design utilize natural elements like wood, stone, water, and greenery, all maintaining a balance with nature. Open-air rooms allow guests to admire the stately Sangre de Cristo Mountains from the warmth of hot-spring baths. These baths are communal and are experienced in the nude, according to Japanese custom, though private tubs are available. In addition to the traditional tubs, the spa features steam rooms, saunas, and private treatment rooms. A variety of facial and body services are available, including massages, facials, and herbal wraps. The Watsu massage, "Four Hands, One Heart" Massage, and Japanese Nightingale Facial are among some of the signature treatments at Ten Thousand Waves. During the Watsu aquatic massage, the guest is cradled in the arms of the therapist (with the face supported above the water) and moved through a series of stretches and deep massage in a body-temperature waterfall tub. Geishas and Kabuki actors have used the Japanese Nightingale Facial, which incorporates aromatherapy and botanicals, for centuries.

SIGNATURE TREATMENT: WATSU AND "FOUR HANDS, ONE HEART" MASSAGE

Das auf das traditionelle japanische *onsen* (heißes Quellbad) spezialisierte Ten Thousand Waves bringt den Osten in den Westen. Obwohl es seinen asiatischen Wurzeln treu bleibt, besitzt es doch das Flair des amerikanischen Südwestens – schließlich liegt es im landschaftlich reizvollen Santa Fe. Architektur und Design sind bewusst minimalistisch gehalten und setzen auf natürliche, umweltverträgliche Elemente wie Holz, Wasser und Grünpflanzen. Durch die halboffenen Räume können die Gäste von den heißen Quellbädern aus die imposanten Sangre-de-Cristo-Berge bewundern. Getreu der japanischen Tradition wird hier nackt und gemeinschaftlich gebadet, auf Wunsch stehen auch private Becken zur Verfügung. Außerdem verfügt das Spa über Dampfräume, Saunas sowie private Behandlungsräume. Das Angebot umfasst zahlreiche Massagen, Gesichtsbehandlungen und Kräuterwickel. Zu den Wellness-Specials des Ten Thousand Waves gehören die Watsu-Massage, die „Vier Hände, ein Herz"-Massage sowie eine Gesichtsbehandlung namens „Japanische Nachtigall". Die Watsu-Massage findet in einem auf Körpertemperatur erwärmten Becken mit Wasserfall statt. Dabei wird der Gast vom Therapeuten so gehalten, dass sein Kopf stets über Wasser bleibt. Es folgt eine Reihe von Dehnübungen und Tiefengewebsmassagen. Die „Japanische Nachtigall", eine Gesichtsbehandlung auf Aromatherapie- und Pflanzenbasis, ist unter Geishas und Kabuki-Darstellern schon seit Jahrhunderten verbreitet.

WELLNESS-SPECIAL: WATSU UND DIE „VIER HÄNDE, EIN HERZ"-MASSAGE

S'inspirant des *onsen* japonais (stations thermales alimentées par des sources chaudes), le Ten Thousand Waves a importé les techniques orientales dans le monde occidental. Fidèle à ses racines asiatiques, le spa possède néanmoins un style rappelant la région de Santa Fe dans laquelle il est implanté. L'architecture minimaliste recourt à des éléments naturels comme le bois, la pierre, l'eau et les plantes, pour former un ensemble, en harmonie avec la nature. Des salles en plein air permettent aux hôtes d'admirer la chaîne Sangre de Cristo tout en savourant la chaleur des bains d'eau thermale. Ces bains sont publics et doivent être pris entièrement nu, conformément à la tradition japonaise. Des bains privés sont cependant disponibles. Outre les bains traditionnels, le spa dispose d'étuves, de saunas et de salles de soins privées où sont pratiqués massages, masques et enveloppements aromatiques. Parmi les spécialités du Ten Thousand Waves figurent le massage watsu, le massage « Quatre mains, un cœur » et le masque japonais du rossignol. Au cours du massage aquatique watsu, le corps est bercé dans les bras d'un thérapeute (la tête étant soutenue à la surface de l'eau) qui effectue une série d'étirements et de massages en profondeur dans un bassin dont l'eau est maintenue à la température du corps. Les geishas et les acteurs de kabuki utilisent le masque japonais du rossignol (à base de plantes et d'huiles essentielles) depuis plusieurs siècles.

SOIN PHARE : WATSU ET MASSAGE « QUATRE MAINS, UN CŒUR »

Ten Thousand Waves
3451 Hyde Park Road
Sante Fe, NM 87501
United States

TEL: +1 505 9925025
FAX: +1 505 9895077
EMAIL: info@tenthousandwaves.com
WEBSITE: www.tenthousandwaves.com

CLAY

An oasis in the heart of New York City, CLAY is a hybrid of health club and spa that offers a comprehensive and holistic approach to health and wellness. The name "CLAY" is all about molding, shaping, and the potential for transformation. Neither purely gym nor spa, CLAY displays elements of both: treadmills, recumbent bikes, free weights, and facilities for Pilates and spinning, as well as yoga studios and massage rooms. The innovative programming offers seminars such as cooking classes and nutritional counseling to help extend your healthy regimen to the kitchen. Exercise classes range from hard-core kick-boxing and boot camp to yoga, swing dancing, Pilates, and meditation. And then there are the post-workout perks: a fireside seating area, drenched in sunlight from the overhead skylight, and the rooftop lounge. CLAY's spa menu includes a bevy of massages: aromatherapy, chair, deep tissue, hot stone, medical, prenatal, reflexology, shiatsu, sports, and Swedish. CLAY tailors its signature aromatherapy massage to concentrate on lowering stress, raising energy, detoxifying, or soothing aches and pains. Each focus uses different plant extracts and essential oils to meet its goals. CLAY's natural face treatments take this same approach, using different skin-care regimens to encourage deep cleaning and regeneration.

SIGNATURE TREATMENT: AROMATHERAPY MASSAGE

Das CLAY ist eine Oase mitten in New York City. Die Mischung aus Health Club und Spa hat sich Gesundheits- und Wellness-Anwendungen verschrieben, die einen ganzheitlichen Ansatz verfolgen. Der Name CLAY (engl. für „Lehm") steht hier für das Formen und Straffen und die Möglichkeit, sich zu verwandeln. Laufbänder, Liegeräder, freie Gewichte und Kursräume für Pilates und Spinning sind hier ebenso zu finden wie Yoga-Studios und Massageräume. Zum innovativen Angebot gehören außerdem Kochkurse und Ernährungsberatung. Kurse in Kick-Boxen und Boot-Camp stehen hier ebenso auf dem Programm wie Pilates- oder Mediationsstunden, Yoga oder Swing-Dancing. Nach dem Workout warten Ruheinseln wie die eingemauerte Sitzbank vor dem Kamin auf die durch ein Oberlicht die Sonne scheint. Auch auf der Dachterrasse lässt es sich herrlich loungen. Das Spa des CLAY bietet eine ganze Reihe von Massagen an: Aromatherapie-, Stuhl-, Tiefengewebsmassage, Massage mit heißen Steinen, medizinische Massagen sowie Massagen für werdende Mütter, Reflexologie, Shiatsu, Sport- und Schwedische Massage. Das Wellness-Special des CLAY, die Aromatherapie-Massage, wirkt wahlweise stressmindernd, belebend, entschlackend oder schmerzlindernd. Je nachdem, welche Wirkung erzielt werden soll, kommen andere Pflanzenextrakte und essenzielle Öle zum Einsatz. Dasselbe gilt für die Gesichtsbehandlungen des CLAY. Um die Haut porentief zu reinigen und zu regenerieren, steht eine ganze Palette von Hautpflegeprodukten zur Auswahl.

WELLNESS-SPECIAL: AROMATHERAPIE-MASSAGE

CLAY, véritable oasis en plein cœur de New York, est à la fois un club de gym et un spa, offrant une approche globale, holistique, de la santé et du bien-être. Le mot «clay» signifie argile, et évoque le modelage, l'évolution, le potentiel de transformation. CLAY dispose de tapis de jogging, de vélos d'appartement, d'haltères, propose des séances de Pilates, de yoga, des massages... Novateurs, les programmes comportent des cours de cuisine et des conseils de nutrition qui permettent d'entretenir sa vitalité à domicile. Les cours proposés vont du kick-boxing au yoga en passant par différentes danses, le Pilates, la méditation et la musculation. Après les séances, il ne faut pas négliger les plaisirs bien mérités : salon doté d'une cheminée et baigné par la lumière du soleil, et lounge au dernier étage. Le spa, quant à lui, offre divers massages : aromathérapique, profond, aux pierres chaudes, médical, prénatal, réflexologique, shiatsu, sportif et suédois. CLAY personnalise son soin phare, le massage aromathérapique, de façon qu'il élimine le stress, ré-énergise, détoxifie ou apaise les douleurs chroniques. Selon l'optique choisie, différents extraits de plantes et différentes huiles essentielles sont utilisés. Le soin du visage suit la même philosophie en faisant appel à différentes méthodes pour atteindre l'objectif : une purification en profondeur, une regénération absolue.

SOIN PHARE : MASSAGE AROMATHÉRAPIQUE

CLAY
25 West 14th Street
New York, NY 10011
United States

TEL: +1 212 2069200
FAX: +1 212 2061780
EMAIL: tmw@insideclay.com
WEBSITE: www.insideclay.com

The Kiawah Island Club's Sasanqua

Golf is the thing on Kiawah Island, but luxury and relaxation are the goals at its elegant spa. Located on an Atlantic barrier island near Charleston, South Carolina, Sasanqua Spa is an idyllic hideaway that overlooks balmy marshes and gently rippling grasses. Named after a variety of camellia prevalent on the island, Sasanqua was created by renowned designer Clodagh, who communed with nature to create this relaxing retreat. Clad in cypress, stucco, and poplar-bark tile, the expansive 9,000-square-foot wood structure suggests tranquility at first glance. Natural materials that perfectly complement the surroundings are used throughout. The spa embraces its locale, making the experience an interior and exterior one. Spa-goers can pause to take in the local bird life, for example, simply by walking outside. Just beyond the impressive scaled-copper-clad front door is a dramatic infinity pool filled with river rocks, encouraging reflection and contemplation. Inside, signature Sasanqua treatments incorporate indigenous ingredients from Kiawah's diverse surroundings, specifically from the garden, the marsh, and the sea. Sasanqua offers traditional spa services along with ayurvedic offerings, stone massage, and a special Golfer's Advantage package, which incorporates a facial and reflexology to provide essential maintenance for the avid golfer.

SIGNATURE TREATMENT: SASANQUA MASSAGE

Auf Kiawah Island dreht sich alles ums Golfspielen, doch im eleganten Spa sind Luxus und Entspannung das Ziel. Das auf einer Atlantikinsel vor Charleston, South Carolina, gelegene Sasanqua Spa ist ein äußerst idyllisches Refugium. Von hier aus hat man einen herrlichen Blick auf die Sumpflandschaft und die sich in der Dünung wiegenden Gräser. Das nach einer auf der Insel vorkommenden Kamelienart benannte Spa wurde von der renommierten Innenarchitektin Clodagh entworfen. Diese schuf eine Anlage, die völlig im Einklang mit der Natur steht. Der mit Gips, Zypressen- und Pappelrinde vertäfelte, nahezu 850 Quadratmeter große Holzbau strahlt Ruhe und Frieden aus. Für ihn wurden ausschließlich natürliche Materialien verkleidete, die sich perfekt in die Landschaft einfügen. Das Spa umarmt die Natur und verwöhnt so Körper und Seele. Wenn die Gäste eine Pause einlegen und die einheimische Vogelwelt beobachten wollen, müssen sie nur einen Schritt ins Freie tun. Gleich hinter der eindrucksvollen Blutbuchen-Lamellentür liegt ein malerischer Naturpool mit Flusskieseln, der zum Meditieren einlädt. Das Spa selbst verwendet einheimische Zutaten, die in den Gärten, Sümpfen oder im Meer vor Kiawah vorkommen. Das Sasanqua bietet traditionelle Kosmetikbehandlungen und Ayurveda-Anwendungen an. Eine Massage mit heißen Steinen und ein Wellness-Paket speziell für Golfer, stehen ebenfalls auf dem Programm.

WELLNESS-SPECIAL: SASANQUA MASSAGE

À Kiawah Island, le golf est presque une religion, mais dans le spa, les mots-clés sont luxe et détente. Situé dans l'Atlantique, au large de Charleson (Caroline du Sud), le spa Sasanqua constitue une retraite idyllique qui domine les bayous parfumés et les hautes herbes qui ondulent sous le vent ; son nom vient d'une variété de camélia qui pousse sur l'île. Sasanqua a été conçu par le designer Clodagh, qui voulait un lieu en communion avec la nature. La structure de bois de près de 850 mètres carrés, aux murs de cyprès, de crépi ou de peuplier, est empreinte de calme et de sérénité. Partout on a choisi des matériaux naturels en harmonie avec le paysage. Le spa épouse la nature pour rendre l'expérience tant intérieure qu'extérieure. Entre les soins, par exemple, il est possible d'aller observer les oiseaux : il suffit de faire quelques pas dehors. Juste devant la porte d'entrée de cuivre aux proportions impressionnantes, une piscine à débordement – le fond tapissé des pierres de la rivière – incite à la méditation, à la contemplation. À l'intérieur, les soins phares utilisent des ingrédients locaux venus du jardin, du bayou et de la mer. En plus des traitements habituels, Sasanqua propose des soins ayurvédiques, des massages aux pierres, et un forfait spécial golfeur qui comprend un soin du visage et des manipulations de réflexologie : l'idéal pour se maintenir en forme.

SOIN PHARE: MASSAGE SASANQUA

The Kiawah Island Club's Sasanqua
10 River Course Lane
Kiawah Island, SC 29455
United States

TEL: +1 843 7685725
FAX: +1 843 7685727
EMAIL: sasanqua@kiawahisland.com
WEBSITE: www.kiawahisland.com

The Spa at Sundance

Sundance, at the base of Utah's Wasatch Range, has served as an escape for artists and nature aficionados since Robert Redford purchased the land in 1969. Since then, Sundance has evolved into an enormous rustic compound with facilities for crafts, snow sports, horse riding, and all-round relaxing. With the growth of the Sundance Film Festival and the Sundance Channel, the resort, with 90–100 rooms and adjoining spa, has developed an elite status with celebrities and artists who seek a natural retreat. But it's clear that Sundance wishes to remain true to its roots. There is nothing cold or uninviting about Sundance. Referred to as a "Hocoka," the Sioux term for a sacred environment to restore the spirit and improve the body, the Spa at Sundance focuses on maintaining a peaceful environment that uses traditional Native American sources in its treatments. The treatments express that aim, with options like the Sundance Stone Massage, which uses warm basalt stones on the body to relax the muscles, each stone representing a different direction, color, animal, and life cycle. Cell phones and pagers are not permitted and the staff enforce a "whisper zone" inside the spa. Even the spa's own phones don't ring – they blink!

SIGNATURE TREATMENT: SUNDANCE STONE MASSAGE

Das im Bundesstaat Utah, am Fuß der Wasatch-Bergkette gelegene Sundance ist ein Refugium für Künstler und Naturliebhaber, seit Robert Redford das Land 1969 erworben hat. Mittlerweile ist ein riesiges Zentrum daraus geworden, in dem man kunsthandwerkliche Fähigkeiten erlernen, Skifahren, Reiten oder sich einfach nur erholen kann. Mit zunehmender Bedeutung des Sundance Filmfestivals und des Sundance-Fernsehkanals wurde das Hotel mit seinen 90–100 Zimmern und dem Spa immer exklusiver. Inzwischen hat es bei Prominenten und Künstlern, die Ruhe in der Natur suchen, fast Kultstatus erreicht. Trotzdem verleugnet Sundance seine Wurzeln nicht. Das Spa, das auch „Hocoka" genannt wird – ein Begriff, mit dem die Sioux-Indianer einen heiligen Ort bezeichneten, an dem sich Seele und Körper entspannen – verbreitet Ruhe und Frieden. Dasselbe Ziel verfolgen auch die Anwendungen, die sich traditioneller indianischer Heilmittel bedienen. Dazu gehört unter anderem die „Sundance-Stone-Massage", bei der heiße Basaltsteine auf den Körper gelegt werden, um die Muskulatur zu entspannen. Dabei steht jeder Stein für eine bestimmte Himmelsrichtung, eine Farbe, ein Tier oder einen Lebenszyklus. Die Mitnahme von Handys und Pagern ist verboten und das Personal achtet strikt darauf, dass innerhalb des Spa nur mit gedämpfter Stimme gesprochen wird. Nicht einmal die Spa-eigenen Telefone klingeln – sie blinken nur!

WELLNESS-SPECIAL: MASSAGE MIT HEISSEN STEINEN

Sundance, au pied de la chaîne de montagne des Wasatch Range, dans l'Utah, est un lieu cher aux artistes et aux amoureux de la nature depuis que Robert Redford a acheté le terrain en 1969. Depuis, Sundance est devenu un immense complexe rustique où l'on peut pratiquer les travaux manuels, les sports d'hiver, l'équitation, et se relaxer en profondeur. En parallèle au développement du Sundance Film Festival et de la chaîne de télévision Sundance Channel, l'hôtel avec 90–100 chambres et son spa ont conquis une clientèle de grand standing, dont beaucoup d'artistes et de célébrités voulant profiter de la nature. Sundance n'a jamais renié la simplicité de la nature ; rien ici de froid ou de distant. Le spa, nommé « Hocoka » – mot sioux qui signifie « lieu sacré » – cherche à régénérer l'esprit et améliorer l'état physique grâce à une atmosphère apaisante et des traitements fidèles aux traditions des Indiens d'Amérique. Ainsi, le soin phare de Sundance utilise du basalte chauffé pour détendre les muscles. Chaque pierre représente une direction, une couleur, un animal ou un cycle vital distinct. Les téléphones portables et les pagers sont interdits, et une « zone de murmure » est mise en place. Ici, même les téléphones fixes ne sonnent pas – ils clignotent !

SOIN PHARE: MASSAGE AUX PIERRES CHAUDES

The Spa at Sundance
Sundance, RR3 Box A-1
Sundance, UT 84604
United States

TEL: +1 801 2254107
FAX: +1 801 2261937
EMAIL: reservations@sundance-utah.com
WEBSITE: www.sundanceresort.com

Amangani

A private, understated property, Amangani, known as "the peaceful home," is Amanresort's first venture in North America. The 40-suite, three-story paradise sits on the edge of a cliff 7,000 feet above sea level, overlooking mountains and the boundless land of the American West. Amangani reflects a blending of indigenous cultural influences and natural contours of the landscape with the rustic elegance of traditional Western style. The mesmerizing views are not limited to the public space. Every room, every bathroom, the health club, restaurant, and even the heated outdoor swimming pool enjoy the same spectacle of the mountains and sunsets of Wyoming. Amangani's use of Oklahoma sandstone, Pacific redwood, Douglas fir, and other native timber gives the resort a rustic grace. The Health Center consists of two exercise studios finished in redwood, four treatment rooms, and separate steam rooms for men and women. The gym offers a variety of one-on-one programs such as aerobics, extensive yoga, and meditation. The hydraulic treatment massage features a bed of contoured cushions specifically designed to comfort sore bodies. Also available are facials and separate mud, salt, and seaweed body treatments, while haircuts, deep conditioning treatments, manicures, and pedicures can be booked in the beauty salon.

SIGNATURE TREATMENT: SEAWEED BODY TREATMENTS

Das kleine Amangani („Hort des Friedens") ist das erste nordamerikanische Hotel der Amanresorts-Kette. Das dreistöckige, 40 Suiten umfassende Paradies thront auf einer 2.100 Meter hohen Klippe. Von hier aus hat man einen herrlichen Blick auf die Berge und die unendliche Weite des amerikanischen Westens. Das Amangani ist eine gelungene Mischung aus ursprünglichen Kulturen, einer beeindruckenden Landschaft und der rustikalen Eleganz des traditionellen Western-Stils. Die atemberaubende Aussicht beschränkt sich nicht nur auf die Gemeinschaftsräume. Jedes Zimmer, jedes Bad, ja auch Health Club, Restaurant und der beheizte Außenpool bieten einen Blick auf die Berge und Sonnenuntergänge Wyomings. Die Verwendung von Oklahoma-Sandstein, Rotholz, Douglas-Fichte und anderen Nadelhölzern verleiht der Anlage eine rustikale Eleganz. Das Health Center besteht aus zwei Übungsräumen, die ganz in Rotholz gehalten sind, vier Behandlungsräumen sowie getrennten Dampfbädern für Männer und Frauen. Das Fitness-Studio bietet eine Reihe von Kursen in Aerobic, Yoga und Meditation an. Für die Wasserdruck-Massage steht eine anatomisch geformte Liege bereit, die erschöpften Gliedern Linderung verschafft. Außerdem werden Gesichtsbehandlungen, Schlammpackungen sowie Ganzkörperbehandlungen mit Meersalz und Algen angeboten. Im hauseigenen Schönheitssalon können Termine beim Friseur, der Kosmetikerin sowie Maniküre- und Pediküre-Sitzungen vereinbart werden.

WELLNESS-SPECIAL: GANZKÖRPERBEHANDLUNGEN MIT ALGEN

Amangani, « la maison paisible », est le premier établissement d'Amanresort en Amérique du nord. Les trois étages de ce paradis de 40 suites dominent les montagnes et l'immensité de l'Ouest américain depuis le sommet d'une falaise de 2 100 mètres. Amangani mêle l'influence culturelle des Indiens à l'élégance rustique des pionniers. Les fabuleux paysages ne sont pas seulement visibles depuis les parties communes ; chaque chambre, chaque salle de bains, la salle de gym, le restaurant et même la piscine intérieure donnent sur les montagnes du Wyoming et leurs célèbres couchers de soleil. Des bois typiques – grès d'Oklahoma, séquoia du Pacifique, sapin Douglas – donnent aux bâtiments un charme champêtre. Le centre de santé comporte deux salles de gym en séquoia, quatre salles de soins et des hammams pour hommes et pour femmes. Des séances individuelles d'aérobic, de yoga et de méditation sont proposés, ainsi que des massages hydrauliques sur un lit anti-douleurs, des soins du visage, des soins à la boue, au sel et aux algues. À l'institut de beauté, coupes de cheveux, soins régénérants, manucure et pédicure complètent les soins.

SOIN PHARE : SOIN DU CORPS AUX ALGUES

Amangani
1535 North East Butte Road
Jackson, WY 83001
United States

TEL: +1 307 7347333
FAX: +1 307 7347332
EMAIL: amangani@amanresorts.com
WEBSITE: www.amanresorts.com

Oceania

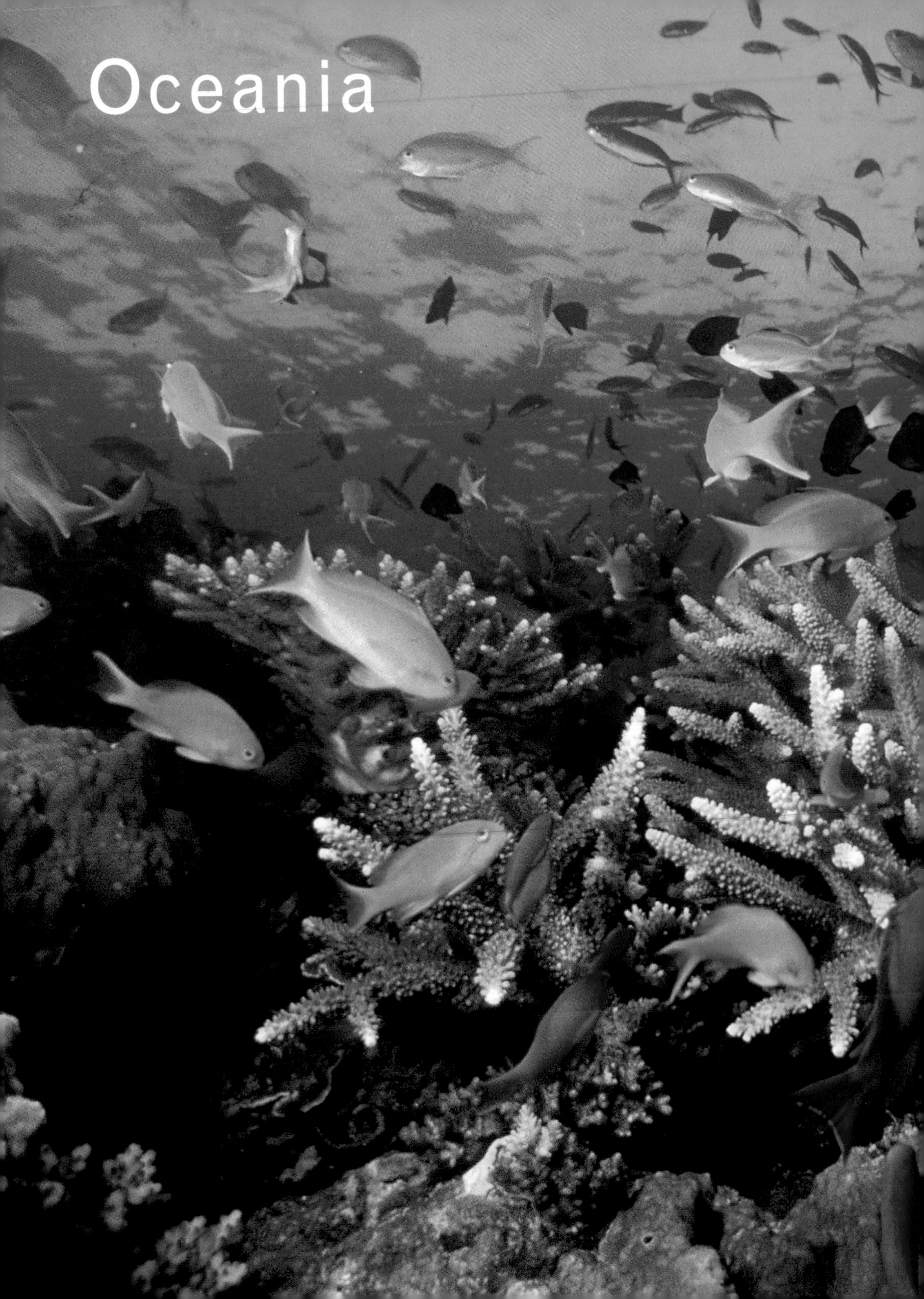

Bedarra Island

The romance of a private island doesn't get much more exclusive than this. At Bedarra Island, the champagne flows freely, sunset canapés are delivered to your pavilion daily, and sprawling daybeds await eager sun-worshippers. It's the most upmarket version of an all-inclusive vacation: guests pay one package price and are free to eat, drink, and pursue resort activities as they wish. Located off the coast of Tropical North Queensland, on the fabled Great Barrier Reef, the 250-acre island comprises pristine rainforest (home to numerous species of birds, butterflies, lizards, and wildlife), secluded beaches with swaying palms, and 16 architecturally stunning villas hidden amid the trees that serve as guest rooms. Two beachfront pavilions overlooking Wedgerock Bay have walls of floor-to-ceiling glass, timber decks with private plunge pools, and oversized bathrooms with deep-soaking tubs and custom-designed "floating" beds. For high-tech access and maximum panoramic views, book the Point, a split-level villa accessed by a private rainforest path and featuring a sizeable living area with a workstation and plasma-screen TV. Massages, facials, and various healing therapies are available in the treatment center overlooking the beach (try the Kodo massage, which incorporates Aboriginal techniques and native essential oils); more extensive pampering is available by taking a 15-minute boat ride to Dunk Island's Spa of Peace and Plenty. Back at Bedarra, the fully stocked, self-serve open bar awaits.

SIGNATURE TREATMENT: KODO MASSAGE

Kaum ein Ort kann diese Privatinsel an Romantik und Exklusivität überbieten: Auf Bedarra Island fließt der Champagner in Strömen. Pünktlich zum Sonnenuntergang werden frische Kanapees zum eigenen Pavillon gebracht und am Strand warten großzügige Liegen auf Sonnenanbeter. Was man hier geboten bekommt, ist All-inclusive der anspruchsvollsten Sorte. Auf der 100 Hektar großen Insel, die vor der Küste des tropischen Nord-Queensland liegt und zum berühmten Great-Barrier-Riff gehört, gibt es unberührten Regenwald in dem zahlreiche Wildtiere leben, einsame Palmenstrände und 16 zwischen Bäumen versteckte Villen für die Gäste. Zwei Strandpavillons mit Blick auf die Wedgerock Bay haben Panoramafenster, Sonnendecks mit eigenem Tauchbecken sowie riesige Bäder mit großzügigen Wannen. Wer Hightech und ein atemberaubendes Panorama wünscht, bucht das Point, eine mehrstöckige Villa mit Workstation und Flachbildfernseher. Massagen, Gesichtsbehandlungen sowie diverse Heiltherapien können im Spa-Center mit Meerblick gebucht werden. (Besonders empfehlenswert ist die Kodo-Massage, die mit Techniken der Aborigines und einheimischen, essenziellen Ölen arbeitet.) Noch mehr verwöhnen lassen kann man sich in dem 15 Bootsminuten entfernten Dunk Island Spa. Zurück auf Bedarra wartet die gut sortierte Freiluft-Bar, an der man sich selbst bedienen kann.

WELLNESS-SPECIAL: KODO-MASSAGE

Difficile de trouver plus luxueux ou plus sélect que l'île de Bedarra. Le champagne coule à flots, les petits fours sont livrés dans chaque bungalow au coucher du soleil, les transats invitent à se prélasser au soleil. Le forfait donne accès aux repas, au bar, et à toutes les activités du complexe. Au large de Tropical North Queensland, sur la légendaire barrière de corail, cette île de 100 hectares est en partie couverte d'une forêt tropicale encore intacte (qui abrite d'innombrables espèces d'oiseaux, de papillons, de lézards et d'animaux sauvages) et bordée de plages vierges et de palmiers. 16 superbes villas se cachent parmi les arbres. En bord de mer, deux pavillons dominant Wedgerock Bay ont des murs transparents, des pontons de bois dotés de piscines privées, et d'immenses salles de bains équipées de bains flottants sur-mesure. Au bout d'un sentier qui serpente dans la forêt, la villa « The Point » offre à la fois une vue panoramique insurpassable et un équipement high-tech (station informatique et télévision à écran plasma). Le centre de soin donne sur la plage et dispense massages, soins du visage, et cures inspirées de diverses traditions (le massage Kodo utilise des techniques aborigènes et des huiles essentielles locales). Des soins encore plus complets attendent au quart d'heure de bateau, au Spa of Peace and Plenty de Dunk Island,. De retour à Bedarra, le bar, largement garni, est fort tentant... et si accueillant !

SOIN PHARE : MASSAGE KODO

Bedarra Island
Via Cairns & Dunk Island
Queensland
Australia

TEL: +61 7 40688233
FAX: +61 7 40688215
EMAIL: travel@voyages.com.au
WEBSITE: www.voyages.com.au

Daintree Eco Lodge & Spa

A forerunner in the ecotourism movement, the Daintree Eco Lodge & Spa features 15 secluded treehouse villas set deep within a lush, tropical 30-acre rainforest canopy. Daintree takes pride in the fact that it incorporates Aboriginal culture and tradition into all aspects of its resort, thus assisting the local Kuku Yalanji people in the relearning and sharing of their ancient culture. Nearly all of the treatments are based on Aboriginal medicines and massage techniques. All utilize products created from Australian flora, earth, sea minerals, and plants, and Daintree's therapists have adapted centuries-old, indigenous holistic healing techniques. Enriching and cleansing treatments include the spa's signature Mala Mayi body treatment, which cocoons the body in warm Mapi mud, followed by "rain therapy" and an optional Kodo full body massage. The pleasant, trance-inducing Bijaaril, or The Dreaming – designed to reconnect the mind, body, and soul – combines foot, scalp, and hand treatment, hydrotherapy, massage, and a facial. Daintree offers a range of activities for guests with an interest in sustainability and the environment, including bird-watching, diving, or snorkeling in the Outer Barrier Reef, and rainforest walks led by local Kuku Yalanji guides. Whether in the spa or in the forest, the focus on integrating nature and indigenous culture is wholly apparent.

SIGNATURE TREATMENT: MALA MAYI BODY TREATMENT

Das Daintree Eco Lodge & Spa ist ein Vorreiter des Ökotourismus. Es besteht aus 15 einsam gelegenen Baumhaus-Villen, über die sich ein tropischer, 15 Hektar umfassender Regenwald-Baldachin wölbt. In Daintree ist man stolz darauf, dass sich Kultur und Traditionen der Aborigines überall niederschlagen. Auf diese Weise unterstützt man den hier ansässigen Stamm der Kuku Ylanji in der Pflege und Weitergabe der alten Kulturtechniken. Fast alle Behandlungen basieren auf den Heil- und Massagetechniken der Aborigines. Man verwendet ausschließlich Produkte, die aus australischer Erde, australischen Meeresmineralien und Pflanzen gewonnen werden. Daintree-Therapeuten haben die Jahrhunderte alten, ganzheitlich orientierten Heiltechniken der Ureinwohner modernen Bedürfnissen angepasst. Zu den pflegenden und reinigenden Anwendungen gehört auch die Mala-Mayi-Ganzkörperbehandlung. Bei diesem Wellness-Special wird man in warmen Mapi-Schlamm gepackt. Anschließend folgt eine „Regentherapie" und auf Wunsch noch eine Kodo-Ganzkörpermassage. Die einen in Trance versetzende Anwendung namens „Bijaaril" bzw. „The Dreaming" dagegen wurde eigens entwickelt, um Körper und Seele ins Gleichgewicht zu bringen. Sie verbindet Behandlungen der Füße, der Kopfhaut und der Hände mit Hydrotherapie, Massage und Gesichtsbehandlungen. Gästen mit Interesse an der Umwelt hat Daintree so Einiges zu bieten: Hier kann man Vögel beobachten, tauchen, vor dem Barrier-Riff schnorcheln oder unter der Leitung erfahrener Führer aus dem Stamm der Kuku Yalanji eine Regenwaldwanderung unternehmen. Ob im Spa oder im Wald – der Respekt vor der Natur und der Kultur der Ureinwohner ist allgegenwärtig.

WELLNESS-SPECIAL: MALA-MAYI-GANZKÖRPERBEHANDLUNG

Précurseur de l'écotourisme, le Daintree Eco Lodge & Spa, comporte 15 maisons perchées dans les arbres d'une forêt tropicale de 15 hectares. Daintree est fier d'avoir incorporé les traditions des aborigènes à l'ensemble du complexe, aidant ainsi la tribu Kuku Yalanji à renouer avec la culture de leur ancêtres. La plupart des traitements sont nés de la médecine et des techniques de massage de ce peuple. Tous utilisent des produits issus de la flore, de la terre et de l'océan australiens, et des spécialistes ont adapté des techniques holistiques séculaires. Parmi les traitements purifiants et nourrissants, le soin phare, un soin du corps Mala Mayi, consiste en un enveloppement de boue chaude Mapi, suivi d'un « soin pluie » et, en option, d'un massage du corps Kodo. Le Rêve, « Bijaaril », permet d'atteindre un état second afin de réconcilier âme, mental et physique : soins des pieds, du crâne et des mains, hydrothérapie, massage, et soin du visage. Daintree propose diverses activités en rapport avec l'environnement, comme l'observation des oiseaux, la plongée avec ou sans bouteilles sur la barrière de corail, et des randonnées dans la forêt tropicale sous la conduite d'un guide kuku yalanji. Dans le spa ou en pleine forêt, le but premier est toujours d'intégrer la culture locale et la nature environnante.

SOIN PHARE : SOIN DU CORPS MALA MAYI

Daintree Eco Lodge & Spa
20 Daintree Road
Daintree, Queensland 4873
Australia

TEL: +61 7 40986100
FAX: +61 7 40986200
EMAIL: info@daintree-ecolodge.com.au
WEBSITE: www.daintree-ecolodge.com.au

Namale

Namale was born from a dream. Owner Tony Robbins and his wife, Becky, sat spellbound one night under a canopy of stars in this remote Fijian village hidden in the South Pacific. From that moment on, the couple vowed to share the area's splendors with the rest of the world – so they built Namale. The resort rests at the edge of the Koro Sea in Fiji, surrounded by rainforest waterfalls. Thirteen bures (quaint cottages with thatched roofs) and two larger villas offer amazing views and private decks. The bures are so comfortable guests may be tempted never to leave their rooms, but to encourage them to appreciate the lush surroundings, Namale offers community activities, including its own Fiji-style bowling alley and scuba diving. Favorite dive spots include Dreamhouse, a pinnacle dive where you can swim among schools of hundreds of fish. Namale's Spa and Sanctuary sits at the edge of a volcanic cliff, and to take advantage of its spectacular vista, was designed with oversized glass walls and a glass-enclosed cliff-top Jacuzzi. Guests can indulge in couples massage, hydrotherapy, aromatherapy, traditional spa treatments, and seaweed wraps. A signature treatment at the resort is the Namale Tandem Massage, featuring two therapists working together.

SIGNATURE TREATMENT: NAMALE TANDEM MASSAGE

Namale ist die Verwirklichung eines Traums: Eines Nachts saßen der Eigentümer Tony Robbins und seine Frau Becky völlig verzaubert in dem einsamen Fiji-Dorf im Südpazifik und betrachteten den Sternenhimmel. In diesem Moment schwor sich das Paar, die herrliche Gegend auch für den Rest der Welt zu erschließen – und errichtete Namale. Die Anlage befindet sich direkt an der Koro-See und ist von Regenwald-Wasserfällen umgeben. Dreizehn malerische, palmblattgedeckte Hütten („bures") sowie zwei größere Villen mit Sonnendecks bieten eine prächtige Aussicht. Die Bures sind so bequem ausgestattet, dass man sie gar nicht mehr verlassen mag. Damit sich die Gäste trotzdem dazu aufraffen, die herrliche Umgebung zu erkunden, bietet Namale zahlreiche Freizeitaktivitäten an: Dazu gehören ein Besuch der Bowlingbahn im Fidji-Stil oder ein Schnorchelausflug. Eines der beliebtesten Tauchparadiese ist das „Dreamhouse", wo man sich inmitten von Fischschwärmen bewegt. Das hauseigene Spa mit Meditationsraum liegt am Rand einer Klippe vulkanischen Ursprungs. Damit man die atemberaubende Aussicht genießen kann, gibt es riesige Panoramafenster und einen verglasten Jacuzzi. Zum Verwöhnangebot gehören eine Massage speziell für Paare, Hydro-, Aromatherapie, traditionelle Spa-Behandlungen und Algenpackungen. Eines der Wellness-Specials von Namale ist die so genannte Tandem-Massage, bei der zwei Therapeuten zusammenarbeiten.

WELLNESS-SPECIAL: NAMALE-TANDEM-MASSAGE

Namale est né d'un rêve. Le propriétaire, Tony Robbins, et son épouse Becky admiraient le ciel étoilé de ce petit village des îles Fidji. Ils se promirent alors de faire partager cette splendeur au reste du monde – et pour cela, édifièrent Namale au bord de la mer de Koro, dans la forêt équatoriale. Les 13 charmants bungalows aux toits de chaume (bures) et les deux villas ont tous une vue superbe, et disposent de pontons privés. Le confort des bures est tel qu'on peut avoir envie d'y passer ses journées, mais les activités proposées sont si tentantes, et le décor tellement idyllique, qu'on n'hésite pas à pratiquer la plongée ou la version locale du bowling. L'une des plus belles zones de plongées est la « dreamhouse », où l'on peut nager au milieu des bancs de poissons. Le spa et le sanctuaire sont situés au bord d'une falaise volcanique ; pour ne rien perdre de la vue spectaculaire, les murs sont en verre et les jacuzzis donnent directement sur l'extérieur. Les soins proposés comprennent massages pour couples, hydrothérapie, aromathérapie, spa traditionnel et enveloppement aux algues. L'un des soins phares est le massage tandem Namale, pour lequel deux praticiens travaillent de concert.

SOIN PHARE : MASSAGE TANDEM NAMALE

Namale
PO Box 244
Savusavu
Fiji Islands

TEL: +679 8850435
FAX: +679 8850400
EMAIL: reservations@namaleresort.com
WEBSITE: www.namalefiji.com

Bora Bora Lagoon Resort

Located on a small island 150 miles northwest of Tahiti, the Bora Bora Lagoon Resort is surrounded by 14 acres of lush tropical green-ery, bordered by a quarter-mile of white-sand beaches, and shadowed by the volcanic peak of Mount Otemanu. The resort's architec-ture takes on a local flair with Polynesian pandanau roofing, Tahitian woods, and paintings by Tahitian artist Garrick Yrondi in the reception area. Guests can choose from 79 garden, beachfront, or over-water Polynesian-style bungalows, each with hardwood floors and open beam ceilings. The resort's signature over-water bungalows feature steps leading from the sundeck directly into the lagoon waters. The resort has ample sports facilities, offers snorkeling, windsurfing, kayaking, helicopter rides, glass-bottom boat trips, shark-feeding excursions, and mountain Jeep safaris. It is renowned for its "motu picnic" – the resort will transport you to a deserted motu island and, while you snorkel or sunbathe, will prepare a fresh lobster barbecue. At the resort, guests can enjoy a traditional massage performed with a local coconut oil called monoi.

SIGNATURE TREATMENT: MONOI OIL MASSAGE

Das Bora Bora Lagoon Resort befindet sich auf einer kleinen Insel, 240 Kilometer nordwestlich von Tahiti. Die Anlage ist von sechs Hektar tropischer Pflanzenwelt umgeben und wird von einem 400 Meter langen, weißen Sandstrand gesäumt. Ganz in der Nähe erhebt sich der Mount Otemanu, ein erloschener Vulkan. Mit seinen polynesischen Bedachungen (*pandanau*), dem Tahiti-Holz und den Gemälden des tahitischen Künstlers Garrick Yrondi, die in der Rezeption hängen, verbreitet die Architektur einheimisches Flair. Die Gäste können zwischen Bungalows mit Meerblick, Bungalows mit Garten oder in polynesischer Pfahlbauweise wählen. Alle Unterkünfte haben Hartholzböden und einen offenen Dachstuhl. Die auf dem Wasser errichteten Pfahlbauten haben den Vorteil, dass ihr Sonnendeck direkt in die Lagune hineinragt. Die Anlage bietet zahlreiche Sportmöglichkeiten wie Schnorcheln, Windsurfen oder Kajak fahren an. Aber auch Hubschrauberflüge, Ausflüge mit dem Glasboden-Boot, Haifütterungs-Exkursionen und Jeepsafaris ins Gebirge stehen auf dem Programm. Etwas ganz Besonderes ist das „Motu-Picknick": Dafür wird der Gast extra auf eine einsame Insel gebracht. Während er schnorchelt oder in der Sonne liegt, wird ein frisches Hummer-Barbecue zubereitet. Zurück im Hotel, können sich die Gäste von einer traditionellen Massage mit dem einheimischen Kokosnussöl namens *monoi* verwöhnen lassen.

WELLNESS-SPECIAL: MONOI-ÖLMASSAGE

Situé sur une petite île à 240 kilomètres au nord-ouest de Tahiti, le Bora Bora Lagoon Resort est entouré de six hectares de végétation tropicale luxuriante, bordé sur 400 mètres de plages de sable blanc et dominé par le pic volcanique du mont Otemanu. De style poly-nésien avec ses toits traditionnels (pandanau), ses bois locaux, et ses peintures dues au pinceau du tahitien Garrick Yrondi qui déco-rent la réception, il offre le choix entre des bungalows situés dans le jardin, sur le front de mer, ou sur pilotis les pieds dans l'eau – mais tous ont des parquets de bois nobles et des plafonds qui s'ouvrent sur le ciel. Les terrasses des bungalows sur pilotis disposent d'une échelle qui plonge dans les eaux du lagon. Les installations sportives et de loisir sont nombreuses – plongée, windsurf, kayak, héli-coptère, sorties à bord de bateaux à fond de verre pour admirer la faune et la flore sous-marines ; on peut également aller nourrir les requins et sillonner les montagnes à bord d'une Jeep. Les « motu pique-nique » sont un délice rare : une fois débarqué sur un îlot désert, on nage ou on bronze pendant que les homards cuisent au barbecue. À l'hôtel, les massages au monoï sont une tradition pré-cieusement perpétuée.

SOIN PHARE : MASSAGE AU MONOÏ

Bora Bora Lagoon Resort
Motu Toopua
BP 175 – 98730 Vaitape
Bora Bora, French Polynesia

TEL: +689 604000
FAX: +689 604001
EMAIL: info@bblr.net
WEBSITE: www.boraboralagoon.com

Esperanza

Cabo San Lucas, Mexico

Barefoot sophistication is the order of the day at Esperanza, a 56-suite resort on the bluffs of Punta Ballena, overlooking Baja's Sea of Cortez. Handcrafted Mexican furnishings, custom-designed rugs, painted floors, and original art fill the rooms, all of which face the water. Guests enter the spa through the spa gruta, a series of steam caves and waterfalls reminiscent of a seaside grotto. The ritual begins with an open-air shower and warm spring soak, followed by a steam, a rinse under a waterfall, and a glass of tropical fruit juice. Inside, sunny colors and rich textures mimic Baja's coastal environment. Antique iron gates lead to each of the seven treatment rooms, which have private gardens and soaking pools shaded by latilla canopies and bougainvillea. (One room has a pool for private watsu treatments.) Ingredients on the spa menu include tropical fruits, desert minerals, and plants of the region. The Papaya Mango Body Polish uses enzyme-rich mashed papaya and mango combined with cornmeal to exfoliate the skin; the Couple's Clay Bake uses a sea algae and clay mask that dries naturally in the sun. Lime-scented linens are used for body wraps, and water misters refresh guests as they rest between treatments.

SIGNATURE TREATMENT: PAPAYA MANGO BODY POLISH

Barfuß-chic wird im Esperanza groß geschrieben. Die 56 Suiten umfassende Anlage befindet sich auf den Klippen der Punta Ballena und bietet einen herrlichen Blick auf die Cortez-See. Handgearbeitete mexikanische Möbel, Teppiche und Böden und jede Menge Kunsthandwerk schmücken die Zimmer mit Meerblick. Die Gäste betreten das Spa durch die „Gruta" – eine Reihe von Dampfhöhlen und Wasserfällen, die an eine Meeresgrotte erinnern. Das Ritual beginnt mit einer Dusche im Freien und einem Bad in der warmen Quelle. Nach dem Schwitzbad im Dampfraum duscht man sich unter dem Wasserfall ab und genießt ein Glas Saft aus tropischen Früchten. Innenräume und Stoffe in sonnigen Farben spiegeln die mexikanische Küstenlandschaft wider. Alte, schmiedeeiserne Tore öffnen sich zu den sieben Behandlungsräumen. Alle verfügen über einen eigenen Garten, Pool und Bougainvillea-Lauben, die angenehmen Schatten spenden. (Zu einem der Behandlungsräume gehört ein separater Watsu-Pool.) Die Spa-Produkte enthalten Wirkstoffe aus tropischen Früchten, Wüstenmineralien und einheimischen Pflanzen. Für das Papaya Mango Body Polish wird ein enzymhaltiger Brei aus den Früchten und Maismehl verwendet. Beim „Clay Bake", einer Behandlung speziell für Paare, wird eine Maske aus Meeresalgen und Tonerde aufgetragen, die an der Sonne trocknen muss. Nach Zitrone duftende Laken umhüllen den Gast bei Bodywraps und zwischen den Anwendungen sorgen Wasserzerstäuber für Erfrischung.

WELLNESS-SPECIAL: PAPAYA MANGO BODY POLISH

Imaginez un hôtel de rêve où « les chaussures restent dans les valises » : vous êtes à Esperanza, un complexe de 56 suites niché sur le promontoire de Punta Ballena surplombant la mer de Cortez, dans l'État de Baja. Mobilier artisanal mexicain, tapis personnalisés, sols peints et autres créations artistiques donnent le ton dans les chambres, qui ont toutes vue sur la mer. L'entrée du spa est constituée d'une enfilade de cavernes et de cascades artificielles évoquant une grotte marine. Le rituel des soins s'ouvre par une douche en plein air et un bain dans une source chaude, se poursuit par un bain de vapeur et un passage sous une cascade d'eau claire, et s'achève avec un verre de délicieux jus de fruits tropicaux. L'intérieur de l'hôtel resplendit de mille couleurs éclatantes et de matières chaudes directement inspirés du décor naturel des côtes de Baja. Chacune des sept salles de soins, accessibles par une lourde porte en fer forgé, dispose de jardins privatifs et de bains à l'ombre des pergolas et des bougainvillées. (Une des salles dispose d'un bassin destiné aux séances individuelles de watsu.) Fruits tropicaux, minéraux du désert et plantes indigènes sont mis en œuvre dans les programmes du spa. Le polissage corporel à la papaye et à la mangue consiste en une exfoliation à base de purée de fruits mêlés à de la semoule de maïs. Le soin spécial Couple's Clay Bake, concocté spécialement pour les couples, consiste en une application d'algues marines et un masque d'argile que l'on laisse sécher naturellement au soleil. Des draps parfumés au citron vert sont utilisés pour les enveloppements. Entre chaque soin, un personnel attentionné propose de l'eau fraîche aux hôtes.

SOIN PHARE : POLISSAGE CORPOREL À LA PAPAYE ET À LA MANGUE

Esperanza
Carretera Transpeninsular Km 7
Cabo San Lucas
Baja California Sur, 23410 Mexico

TEL: +52 624 1456400
FAX: +52 624 1456499
EMAIL: reservations@esperanzaresort.com
WEBSITE: www.esperanzaresort.com

Las Ventanas al Paraíso

At the tip of the Baja Peninsula, where the Sea of Cortez meets the Pacific, Las Ventanas al Paraíso embodies Mexico's rich architectural heritage. Smooth adobe walls and hand-carved cedar doors lead to 61 expansive guest suites with platform beds, stone floors with inlaid-pebble work, and wood-burning terracotta fireplaces. Vibrant paintings, pottery, and murals fill interiors with color, while a series of ponds and infinity-edge swimming pools echo the deep blue colors of the sea. Spa treatments draw from the Tepezcohuite techniques used by ancient Mayans, as well as other holistic therapies and rituals – from phytotherapy to plant medicine. The Tepezcohuite healing wrap is indigenous to Chiapas, used in severe cases of sunburn and sun blisters; the Desert Purification treatment, in which volcanic clay is used to exfoliate and detoxify, was inspired by Aztec and Mayan ceremonies. Acupuncture, vibrational healing, raindrop therapy, and ayurvedic treatments are also on offer. Massages can be performed in the beach pavilion, or on board the resort's 55-foot yacht; the spa even offers stress-reducing neck massages for pets. At night, an aromatherapy turndown service allows guests to select from a menu of essential oils – from stress-relieving to exuberance-balancing – which are then burned in small chimneys by the bed.

SIGNATURE TREATMENT: DESERT PURIFICATION

An der Spitze der Halbinsel Baja, wo die Cortez-See auf den Pazifik trifft, spiegelt das Luxushotel Las Ventanas al Paraíso Mexikos reiches kulturelles Erbe wider. Hinter glatten Lehmziegelwänden und handgeschnitzten Türen aus Zedernholz finden sich 61 geräumige Suiten, die mit Steinböden und Kiesel-Intarsien sowie Terrakotta-Feuerstellen, in denen Holzscheite knistern, ausgestattet sind. Lebhafte Bilder, Keramik und Wandgemälde bringen Farbe in die Inneneinrichtung, während eine Reihe von Becken und Naturpools mit dem Blau des Ozeans wetteifern. Die Spa-Anwendungen reichen von den Tepezcohuite-Techniken der alten Mayas bis hin zu anderen ganzheitlichen Therapien und Ritualen. Die Tepezcohuite-Heilwickelbehandlung stammt aus Chiapas und ist besonders bei Sonnenbrand oder Sonnenallergie zu empfehlen. Die „Desert Purification", bei der mithilfe von Vulkanschlamm gepeelt und entgiftet wird, orientiert sich an alten Ritualen der Azteken und Mayas. Akupunktur, Resonanzheilung, Regentropfentherapie und Ayurveda gehören ebenfalls zum Angebot. Massieren lassen kann man sich im Strandpavillon oder an Bord der hoteleigenen 17-Meter-Yacht. Das Spa bietet sogar entspannende Nackenmassagen für Haustiere an. Vor dem Einschlafen gibt es eine Aromatherapie. Dafür können die Gäste aus zahlreichen Duftessenzen wählen, die Stress abbauen oder für mehr Ausgeglichenheit sorgen. Diese Öle verdunsten dann in kleinen Duftlampen direkt neben dem Bett.

WELLNESS-SPECIAL: DESERT PURIFICATION

À la pointe de la péninsule de Baja, là où la mer de Cortez rencontre le Pacifique, Las Ventanas al Paraíso déploie toutes les richesses du patrimoine architectural mexicain. Derrière les portes en bois de cèdre sculptées à la main des 61 suites spacieuses se trouvent futons, sols pavés ornés de motifs incrustés de galets, cheminées en terracotta. Tandis que l'intérieur des lieux, décoré de peintures majestueuses, de poteries artisanales et de fresques, resplendit de mille couleurs, à l'extérieur, une série de piscines à débordement décline les tons bleu profond de l'océan. Les soins sont inspirés des techniques mayas, ou encore de diverses thérapies holistiques comme la phytothérapie ou les préparations à base de plantes médicinales. Les enveloppements à l'écorce de tepezcohuite – arbre indigène du Chiapas, littéralement «arbre de la peau» – constituent un baume cicatrisant contre les coups de soleils et les brûlures sévères. Quant à la Purification du désert, il s'agit d'une application d'argile volcanique aux vertus exfoliantes et détoxifiantes inspirée des cérémonies aztèques et mayas. Le programme comprend également des séances d'acupuncture, de médecine vibratoire, d'aromathérapie ainsi que des traitements ayurvédiques. Les massages sont prodigués au choix dans un pavillon de plage ou à bord du yacht de 17 mètres appartenant à l'hôtel. Même nos amis quadrupèdes peuvent bénéficier d'un massage antistress du cou. Au coucher, le personnel de chambre propose une sélection d'huiles essentielles aux vertus équilibrantes et relaxantes, qui sont brûlées dans de petites niches près du lit.

SOIN PHARE: PURIFICATION DU DÉSERT

Las Ventanas al Paraíso
Carretera Transpeninsular Km 19.5
San Jose del Cabo
Baja California Sur 23400, Mexico

TEL: +52 624 1442800
FAX: +52 624 1442801
EMAIL: lasventanas@rosewoodhotels.com
WEBSITE: www.lasventanas.com

Hotelito Desconocido

The Hotelito Desconocido is that rare creature of the resort world – a harmonious balance of luxury and ecological purity, pampering and primitive beauty, set amid a wetland preserve for sea turtles and 150 species of birds. Nestled along the Costa Alegre, between the Pacific Ocean and the Sierra Madre Mountains (60 miles south of Puerto Vallerta), the solar-powered Hotelito was conceived by Marcello Murzilli as a place to celebrate rather than contain nature. It is built along the lines of an old Mexican fishing village, and the 29 accommodations in rooms and suites are in simple but lovely palafitos – airy bungalows built on stilts to overlook the edge of the estuary. To arrive at sunset is to enter a magical world, where hundreds of candles, torches, and luminaries conspire with the stars to light the buildings and pathways that meander through the grounds, the setting for the spa, known as "El Mundo de la Salud." After a day of riding horses along the beach or biking through palm groves, an al fresco aromatherapy massage or stone therapy (alternating warm river rocks with cool marble stones) releases stressed muscles. And the restorative Mermaid Bath draws upon local ingredients – sea salts and botanical essential oils – to smooth away dead skin, cleanse toxins, and massage skin back to a natural glow.

SIGNATURE TREATMENT: MERMAID BATH

Das Hotelito Desconocido schafft nicht nur den Spagat zwischen Luxus und Umweltbewusstsein, verschwenderischen Pflegeprogrammen und natürlicher Schönheit, sondern liegt außerdem mitten in einem Naturschutzgebiet für Meeresschildkröten und 150 Vogelarten. Das komplett mit Sonnenenergie betriebene Hotelito schmiegt sich zwischen Pazifik und Sierra Madre an die Costa Alegre. Konzipiert wurde es von Marcello Murzilli, der einen Ort schaffen wollte, an dem man der Natur huldigt, anstatt sie zu zähmen. Die im Stil eines alten mexikanischen Fischerdorfs errichtete Anlage mit 29 Zimmern und Suiten besteht aus schlichten, aber umso hübscheren „palafitos" – geräumigen auf Pfählen errichteten Bungalows, von denen aus man den Meeresarm überblicken kann. Wer bei Sonnenuntergang anreist, erlebt eine magische Welt: Hunderte von Kerzen, Fackeln und Lichter funkeln mit den Sternen um die Wette und beleuchten Gebäude und Wege. Wer den Tag mit Ausritten am Strand oder Radtouren durch die Palmenhaine verbracht hat, freut sich auf eine Aromatherapie-Massage im Freien. Oder aber man genießt eine Massage, bei der abwechselnd warme Flusskiesel und kühler Marmor eingesetzt werden, um verhärtete Muskeln zu entspannen. Beim erholsamen Meerjungfrau-Bad kommen ausschließlich einheimische Zutaten wie Meersalze und essenzielle Pflanzenöle zum Zug, die abgestorbene Hautschuppen entfernen, den Körper entgiften und die Haut durch eine Massage wieder zum Strahlen zu bringen.

WELLNESS-SPECIAL: MEERJUNGFRAU-BAD

L'hôtel Desconocido est une rareté dans le monde des hôtels. Niché dans un écrin de nature, véritable sanctuaire aquatique abritant tortues de mer et quelques 150 espèces protégées d'oiseaux, l'établissement offre un équilibre harmonieux entre luxe hôtelier et préservation de l'écosystème, entre soins haut de gamme et beauté brute de la nature. Construit sur la Costa Alegre, entre l'océan Pacifique et les montagnes de la Sierra Madre (à moins de 100 kilomètres au sud de Puerto Vallarta), l'Hotelito, alimenté par l'énergie solaire, fut conçu par Marcello Murzilli. À l'emplacement d'un ancien village de pêcheurs, ses appartements avec 29 chambres et suites sont de simples mais coquets bungalows sur pilotis – les *palafitos* – dominant les rives de l'estuaire. L'arrivée au coucher du soleil est une expérience unique : des centaines de bougies, de torches et de lumignons semblent avoir conclu un pacte avec les étoiles pour illuminer les bâtiments et les allées sinueuses qui mènent vers le parc du spa, le bien-nommé « El Mundo de la Salud ». Après une randonnée à cheval le long de la plage ou une excursion à vélo à travers les palmeraies, les tensions musculaires disparaîtront sous l'effet bienfaisant d'un massage aux huiles essentielles ou d'une séance de Stone thérapie (applications alternées de galets chauds et de pierres de marbre froides). Le revigorant Bain de la sirène fait appel aux ingrédients indigènes, comme des sels marins et des huiles essentielles à base de plantes locales, pour éliminer les peaux mortes et les toxines, et masser la peau en douceur pour lui redonner son éclat naturel.

SOIN PHARE : BAIN DE LA SIRÈNE

Hotelito Desconocido
Sur de Puerto Vallarta
Playón de Mismaloya
Puerto Vallarta, 48380 Mexico
Mexico

TEL: +52 322 2814010
FAX: +52 322 2814030
EMAIL: hotelito@hotelito.com
WEBSITE: www.hotelito.com

Maroma Resort & Spa

The Maroma Resort and Spa sits in the middle of the Yucatan Peninsula's Riviera Maya, considered to be one of the world's top beaches. Maroma's 58 suites are decadent in their design – mahogany, cedrella, caoba, and ironwood furniture, cashmere throws, and linen slipcovers unite to create a clean, classic decor. The soft blues, taupes, and ivories used throughout create a tranquil yet casual ambience. Maroma's most striking feature is the Mexican Caribbean beach, the prime location for activities such as snorkeling, sailing, and swimming with dolphins. Maroma's complete spa program complements these high-energy activities by providing a well-rounded offering of treatments. Those looking for a good massage can choose from massages tailored to be relaxing or therapeutic, and they can be experienced in the private beachfront areas. Guests can also utilize the spa's flotation chambers, and receive facials, body scrubs, reiki, and aromatherapy. The Temazcal is an hour-and-a-half session that takes place in a underground pyramid where a therapist performs bodywork and massage. It is a ritual of spiritual cleansing, allowing one to sweat away toxins in an ancient sweat lodge.

SIGNATURE TREATMENT: TEMAZCAL TREATMENT

Das Maroma Resort & Spa liegt in der Mitte der Yucatan-Halbinsel, direkt an der Riviera Maya, einem der schönsten Strände der Welt. Die 58 Suiten sind erstklassig ausgestattet – Möbel aus Mahagoni, Zedern-, Caoba- und Eisenholz, Tagesdecken aus Kaschmir und Leinenbettwäsche fügen sich zu einem geschmackvollen, klassischen Dekor. Die gedämpften Blau-, Grau- und Elfenbeintöne der Einrichtung sorgen für ein ruhiges und entspanntes Ambiente. Mit das Attraktivste am Maroma ist jedoch der mexikanisch-karibische Strand – ein idealer Ort, um zu schnorcheln, zu segeln oder mit den Delfinen zu schwimmen. Ergänzt werden diese sportlichen Aktivitäten durch das hauseigene Spa und sein reichhaltiges Behandlungsangebot. Wer sich nach einer guten Massage sehnt, hat die Wahl zwischen entspannenden oder therapeutischen Anwendungen. Sie alle können in Privatkabinen direkt am Strand genossen werden. Außerdem stehen den Gästen Flotation-Räume zur Verfügung. Möglich sind auch Gesichtsbehandlungen, Ganzkörper-Peelings, Reiki und Aromatherapie. Die Temazcal-Behandlung ist eine eineinhalbstündige Sitzung, die in einer unterirdischen Pyramide stattfindet. Bei diesem spirituellen Reinigungsritual entschlackt der Gast in einem alten Schwitztempel und wird von einem Therapeuten gepflegt und massiert.

WELLNESS-SPECIAL: TEMAZCAL-BEHANDLUNG

Le complexe thermal Maroma est idéalement situé sur la Riviera Maya, dans la péninsule du Yucatan, considérée par beaucoup comme l'une des plus belles plages au monde. Les matériaux de décoration sobres et classiques – mobilier en acajou, cèdre, caoba et bois de fer (Olneya tesota), jetées de lit en cachemire et housses en lin – habillent les 58 chambres d'une subtile touche de décadence. L'ambiance sereine et décontractée des lieux est rehaussée par les tons bleus, gris et ivoire omniprésents. Le clou de Maroma est sans aucun doute la plage paradisiaque digne des plus belles cartes postales, qui invite à de nombreuses activités nautiques comme la plongée, la voile ou la nage en compagnie des dauphins. Après une journée d'efforts physiques, quoi de plus agréable qu'un bon massage – relaxant ou thérapeutique – sur un coin de plage privé ? Le spa, quant à lui, propose un programme complet de soins : bain flottant, massage facial, gommage du corps, reiki et aromathérapie. Quant au Tezmacal, il s'agit d'un rituel ancestral de purification et de détoxication par la transpiration. La séance, d'une durée d'une heure et demie, s'accompagne d'un massage prodigué par un thérapeute et a lieu dans une étuve souterraine typique en forme de pyramide.

SOIN PHARE : TEMAZCAL

Maroma Resort & Spa
Carretera Cancún Tulum Km 51
Riviera Maya, Solidaridad,
CP 77710, Mexico

TEL: +52 998 8728200
FAX: +52 998 8728220
EMAIL: reservations@maromahotel.com
WEBSITE: www.orient-expresshotels.com

Verana

Set deep on a hillside in Yelapa, Mexico, with panoramic views of the Pacific Ocean and the mountains of the Valle del Sierra Oriental, Verana is an intimate resort just 20 minutes south of Puerta Vallarta. But you'll feel worlds away in the seclusion of Verana's six unique guesthouses. All six are set within verdant tropical gardens and combine indigenous construction with a modern design sensibility. The spa offers treatments inspired by the surrounding landscape, like the Verana Bath Escapes, a decadent combination of aroma and hydrotherapy under the stars, and the Jungle Facial, which incorporates delectable ingredients such as grapefruit, cucumber, aloe, and orange. More relaxation can be experienced in Verana's beautiful springwater pool with its 180-degree view of the mountains and sea or in your own private hammock. In addition, Verana offers a wide array of activities and excursions including ocean kayaking, fishing, whale and bird watching, trekking, and snorkeling. Cuisine at Verana is inspired by the fresh organic produce grown on the premises – mangos, bananas, papayas, coconuts, pineapples – and is inspired by traditional pre-Hispanic cooking. A full complement of the finest tequilas is also available – as if you needed to take the edge off all that relaxation!

SIGNATURE TREATMENT: VERANA BATH ESCAPES

Das in Yelapa, Mexiko, an einem Hang gelegene Verana bietet eine herrliche Aussicht auf den Pazifik und die Berge des Valle del Sierra Oriental. Die kleine Anlage ist gerade einmal 20 Minuten von Puerta Vallarta entfernt. Trotzdem fühlt man sich in der Abgeschiedenheit des Hotels wie in einer anderen Welt. Alle sechs Gästehäuser liegen in üppigen tropischen Gärten und bieten eine gelungene Kombination aus traditionellem und modernem Design. Auch die Spa-Anwendungen sind von der hiesigen Landschaft geprägt. Eine davon nennt sich Verana Bath Escapes. Das ist eine verschwenderische Kombination von Aroma- und Hydrotherapie unter dem Sternenhimmel, gefolgt von einer Gesichtsbehandlung namens „Jungle". Dabei werden so köstliche Zutaten wie Grapefruit, Gurke, Aloe Vera und Orange verwendet. Wer will, kann sich auch im herrlichen Quellwasser-Pool oder der eigenen Hängematte entspannen. Damit es niemandem langweilig wird, bietet das Verana eine Fülle von Aktivitäten und Ausflügen an wie Kajak fahren, Angeln, Wal- und Vogelbeobachtung, Trekking oder Schnorcheln. Die Küche des Hotels ist von frischen Bioprodukten wie Mangos, Bananen, Papayas, Kokosnüssen und Ananas geprägt, die auf dem Hotelgelände angebaut werden. Die Speisekarte weist eindeutig Einflüsse der traditionellen indianischen Küche auf. Selbstverständlich steht auch eine große Auswahl der besten Tequilas zur Verfügung – schließlich soll man es mit der Wellness nicht übertreiben!

WELLNESS-SPECIAL: VERANA BATH ESCAPES

Niché à flanc de colline au-dessus de Yelapa, petit village de pêcheurs mexicain, Verana offre une vue panoramique sur l'océan Pacifique et les montagnes de la Valle del Sierra Oriental. Dans l'un des ses six pavillons privés, on se sent vraiment à l'écart du monde, bien que l'hôtel ne soit situé qu'à 20 minutes au sud de Puerta Vallarta. Noyée dans un écrin de végétation tropicale, chaque résidence est unique, combinant architecture autochtone et design contemporain. Les soins proposés par le spa s'inspirent de la nature environnante, comme l'insolite Verana Bath Escape, programme combiné d'aromathérapie et hydrothérapie prodigué sous les étoiles, ou encore le Jungle Facial, soin du visage mettant en œuvre de délicieux ingrédients comme le pamplemousse, le concombre, l'aloé et l'orange. Depuis la ravissante piscine d'eau de source de l'hôtel ou le hamac des terrasses privées, la vue embrasses l'infini de la mer et des montagnes. L'établissement propose également un vaste programme d'activités physiques et d'excursions : kayak sur l'océan, pêche, observation des baleines et des oiseaux, trekking et plongée sous-marine. Le menu du restaurant, inspiré par la cuisine préhispanique, fait une large place aux produits frais cultivés sur place : mangues, bananes, noix de coco, ananas, etc. Pour finir la soirée, une sélection de tequilas de premier choix prépare au sommeil de la manière la plus délicieuse.

SOIN PHARE : BAIN AROMATHÉRAPIQUE AU CLAIR DE LUNE

Verana
Calle Zaragoza No. 404, Colonia Centro
Puerto Vallarta, Jalisco 48304
Mexico

TEL: +1 310 360 0155
FAX: +1 310 360 0158
EMAIL: reservations@verana.com
WEBSITE: www.verana.com

Explora en Patagonia

An oasis in the lush and rugged environs of Chile, Explora en Patagonia will satisfy your extreme adventure urges while pandering to your every five-star desire. The beyond scenic Torres Del Paine National Park with its extreme glacial peaks and abundant flora and fauna is worth the trip. As the hotel owners explain, "We are connoisseurs of our own land and its nature... an unexplored territory, a place to find the secrets of the remote." Explora en Patagonia views the world as a place filled with the secrets and marvels of nature and invites its guests to discover them. Hiking, trekking, and riding are available. After a day spent taking in the splendor of the glacier-fed lakes and jagged snow-covered peaks, treat yourself to open-air Jacuzzi, invigorating sauna, massage, or a dip in the indoor heated pool at the Casa del Baños del Ona. This 28-room "eco-lodge" beyond compare encourages its guests to investigate the natural environment of remote regions of Chile, be challenged (if they want to be), and then return at the end of the day to luxury in the form of comfy feather beds, gourmet cuisine, and relaxing Swedish massages.

SIGNATURE TREATMENT: SWEDISH MASSAGE

Als Oase in der ebenso üppigen wie wilden Landschaft Chiles, kommt das Explora en Patagonia extremer Abenteuerlust ebenso entgegen wie dem Bedürfnis nach Fünf-Sterne-Komfort. Allein schon der faszinierende Nationalpark Torres Del Paine mit seinen extremen Gletschern und der reichen Flora und Fauna ist eine Reise wert. Nach den Worten der Hoteleigentümer – ausgewiesene Kenner von Land und Natur – begreift das Explora en Patagonia die Welt als Hort voller Wunder und Geheimnisse, die zur Erkundung einladen. Auf Wunsch können Wander- und Trekkingtouren sowie Ausritte zu Pferd gebucht werden. Wer tagsüber Gletscher-Seen und schneebedeckte Gipfel bestaunt hat, sollte sich anschließend im Freiluft-Jacuzzi belohnen oder in der Sauna und bei der Massage neue Kräfte tanken. Oder er besucht das beheizte Hallenbad in der Casa del Baños del Ona. Diese unvergleichliche „Öko-Lodge" mit 28 Zimmern ermutigt ihre Gäste, die Naturschönheiten Chiles zu entdecken und, falls gewünscht, bis an ihre Grenzen zu gehen. Nur um sie dann am Ende eines langen Tages mit Daunenbetten, Feinschmeckerküche und entspannenden Schwedischen Massagen zu verwöhnen.

WELLNESS-SPECIAL: SCHWEDISCHE MASSAGE

Oasis de verdure en plein cœur de la sauvage Patagonie, Explora en Patagonia combine sensations fortes pour amoureux de l'extrême et confort ultime digne des plus grands établissements de luxe. Le parc national Torres Del Paine, avec ses glaciers d'altitude et sa faune et sa flore d'une richesse extraordinaire, offre un décor naturel à couper le souffle. Comme l'explique le propriétaire de l'hôtel, fin connaisseur de la région, la Patagonie est une terre de confins, une nature secrète qui renferme bien des merveilles à explorer. Le programme de découverte proposé par l'établissement comprend des excursions à pied ou à cheval, ainsi que des parcours de trekking. Après une journée passée à admirer les lacs de glaciers et les pics déchiquetés recouverts de neige, c'est un pur bonheur que de se délasser dans le jacuzzi en plein air, de se revigorer dans la sauna, de plonger dans la piscine intérieure chauffée où encore de s'abandonner à un massage relaxant à la Casa del Baños del Ona. Pour les inconditionnels de la nature et de l'aventure, Explora avec 28 chambres est une expérience unique. Sur cette terre des extrêmes aux confins du Chili, le vrai luxe est de retrouver, au retour d'une rude expédition, le confort douillet d'un lit de plumes, les plaisirs d'une cuisine raffinée ou la volupté d'un massage suédois.

SOIN PHARE: MASSAGE SUÉDOIS

Explora en Patagonia
Sector Salto Chico Sn
Puerto Natales
Chile

TEL: +56 2 206 6060
FAX: +56 2 228 4655
EMAIL: reservexplora@explora.com
WEBSITE: www.explora.com

Explora en Atacama

Located on the edge of San Pedro de Atacama in the neighborhood of Ayllu de Larache, Explora en Atacama sits on 42 acres of rugged Chilean landscape. The property has 50 rooms and a main building constructed from an old adobe house that features a bar with natural fruit juice and tea. In 2004, Atacama opened Casa del Agua, a spa with open-air wells that feed on deep water. There are two saunas and two steam-bath rooms on the premises as well as treatment rooms for the spa's inventive line of treatments. Explora also has its own line of oils, salts, creams, and body treatment products, whose main ingredients are local herbs and minerals. Casa del Agua's treatments include mud treatment, aromatherapy, hydrotherapy, relaxation massages, gemotherapy, yoga, and Atacaman massages. The Explora philosophy is one of environmental immersion through active adventure. The management provides guests with expert guides to facilitate exploring throughout the gorgeous location. Hikes, photographic safaris, mountain biking, and even volcano tours are all available options.

SIGNATURE TREATMENT: ATACAMAN MASSAGE

Das Hotel am Rande von San Pedro de Atacama bei Ayllu de Larache gelegene Anwesen umfasst 17 Hektar wilder chilenischer Landschaft. Der Besitz besteht aus 50 Zimmern und einem Gemeinschaftsraum, für den ein alter Adobe-Ziegelbau umgebaut wurde. Darin ist eine Bar untergebracht, in der naturbelassene Säfte und Tee serviert werden. Im Jahr 2004 wurde die Casa del Agua eingeweiht, ein Spa mit grundwassergespeisten Freiluft-Becken. Zwei Saunas, zwei Dampfbäder und Behandlungsräume für die originellen Anwendungen gehören ebenfalls mit dazu. Das Explora bietet eine eigene Pflegeserie (Öle, Salze, Cremes und andere Körperpflegemittel) an, die hauptsächlich aus einheimischen Kräutern und Mineralien hergestellt wird. Zu den Behandlungen der Casa del Agua gehören Schlammpackungen, Aroma-, Hydrotherapie, Entspannungsmassagen, Heilkristalltherapie, Yoga sowie die Atacama-Massagen. Die Philosophie des Explora bewegt sich zwischen dem Wunsch nach Einswerden mit der Natur und Abenteuerlust. Auf Wunsch stellt die Hotelleitung den Gästen erfahrene Führer zur Seite, mit denen sie die herrliche Umgebung erkunden können. Wandertouren, Fotosafaris, Mountainbik-Touren, ja sogar Vulkanwanderungen gehören zum Angebot.

WELLNESS-SPECIAL: ATACAMA-MASSAGE

Situé en bordure de San Pedro de Atacama, entre l'océan Pacifique et la Cordillère des Andes, Explora en Atacama se déploie sur 17 hectares de terre sauvage dans le désert chilien d'Atacama. L'établissement compte 50 chambres et un bâtiment principal en pisé où l'on trouve un bar proposant de délicieux jus de fruits frais et une sélection de thés. En 2004, la maison a ouvert la Casa del Agua, un spa disposant de bassins en plein air alimentés par des puits artésiens, de deux saunas et deux hammams, ainsi que de plusieurs salles où sont prodigués divers soins originaux. L'hôtel propose également sa propre ligne d'huiles, de sels, de crèmes et de produits de soin pour le corps à base de plantes et de minéraux de la région. Les traitements thérapeutiques comprennent des applications de boue, des séances d'aromathérapie, d'hydrothérapie, de gemmothérapie, de yoga, de massage relaxant et de massage atacaman. Pour les amoureux de l'aventure, l'établissement offre un programme d'activités fondé sur le principe de l'immersion totale dans l'environnement naturel. Des guides expérimentés proposent des excursions à la découverte des paysages exceptionnels tout proches, dont l'exploration de volcans. Randonnées pédestres, safaris-photos et sorties en mountain-bike sont également au programme.

SOIN PHARE: MASSAGE ATACAMAN

Explora en Atacama
Ayllú de Larache
San Pedro de Atacama
Chile

TEL: +56 2 206 6060
FAX: +56 2 228 4655
EMAIL: reservexplora@explora.com
WEBSITE: www.explora.com

Four Seasons Resort Carmelo

Tucked away in a South American pine forest, the Four Seasons Resort and Spa in Carmelo, Uruguay, provides a full sensory experience for its guests. Carmelo is an authentic South American town that has yet to be overly influenced by tourism. The resort's Asian-inspired spa treatments seek to restore the yin and yang of the universe, providing a balancing environment that links man and woman, sun and moon, sight and touch. The use of salt, seaweed, Uruguayan wine, and sesame honey in body treatments unites this pan-Asian atmosphere with its South American location. The Spa treatments are inspired by the hotel's name, the Four Seasons. One treatment, for example, a full body experience, involves four different massage and fragrance combinations designed to evoke the consecutive sensations of winter, spring, summer, and fall. Other signature treatments include the appropriately titled South American Beat, which includes deep tissue massage to South American music, while Asian Blend uses the therapist's own body weight rather than muscular force for the transmission of pressure, or energy, creating a highly therapeutic effect. Though intimately scaled with just 44 bungalows, the Resort Carmelo boasts a championship golf course, facilities for riding, tennis, and water sports, a health club and spa, and fishing on the Rio de la Platya.

SIGNATURE TREATMENT: SILK WINE TREATMENT

Das versteckt in einem südamerikanischen Pinienwald liegende Four-Seasons-Hotel Carmelo, verwöhnt seine Gäste nach Strich und Faden. Carmelo ist ein ursprünglich gebliebenes, südamerikanisches Städtchen, das vom Massentourismus bislang verschont blieb. Die asiatisch-inspirierten Spa-Behandlungen bemühen sich, Yin und Yang ins Gleichgewicht zu bringen, und schaffen ein Ambiente, in dem Mann und Frau, Sonne und Mond, Sehen und Fühlen zusammenfinden. Durch den Einsatz von Meersalz, Algen, uruguayanischem Wein und Sesamhonig wird eine Verbindung zwischen fernöstlichen Einflüssen und der südamerikanischen Umgebung hergestellt. Die Spa-Behandlungen sind vom Namen des Hotels – „Vier Jahreszeiten" – inspiriert: Eine der Ganzkörperbehandlungen besteht aus vier verschiedenen Aromatherapie-Massagen, die Winter, Frühling, Sommer und Herbst heraufbeschwören. Ein anderes Wellness-Special trägt den sinnigen Namen „South American Beat": Dahinter verbirgt sich eine Tiefengewebsmassage zu südamerikanischen Rhythmen. Beim „Asian Blend" dagegen arbeitet der Therapeut weniger mit Muskelkraft als mit seinem eigenen Körpergewicht, um heilsamen Druck auszuüben. Obwohl das Carmelo mit seinen 44 Bungalows eher klein ist, verfügt es über einen 18-Loch-Championship-Golfplatz, Reitmöglichkeiten, Tennisplatz, Wassersportmöglichkeiten sowie Health Club und Spa. Wer möchte, kann auch auf dem Rio de la Plata angeln.

WELLNESS-SPECIAL: SEIDE-WEIN-BEHANDLUNG

Perdu dans une immense forêt de pins et d'eucalyptus d'Amérique du Sud, le Four Seasons Resort Carmelo décline toute une gamme de plaisirs sensoriels. Carmelo est une authentique ville sud-américaine encore préservée du tourisme de masse. Le programme de soins proposé par le spa est d'inspiration asiatique : il cherche à rétablir l'harmonie cosmique du Yin et du Yang dans un environnement équilibré reliant l'homme et la femme, le Soleil et la Lune, la vue et le toucher. La mise en œuvre du sel, des algues, du vin uruguayen et du miel de sésame dans les traitements corporels réunit l'atmosphère panasiatique et l'environnement sud-américain. Le traitement intégral inspiré par le nom de l'hôtel – « Quatre Saisons » – consiste en quatre massages différents évoquant la succession des quatre saisons de l'année. Parmi les autres massage, le Rythme sud-américain comprend un massage des tissus profonds sur fond de musique traditionnelle, tandis que le Mélange asiatique fait appel au poids du thérapeute plutôt qu'à la force musculaire pour transmettre l'énergie et créer un effet thérapeutique efficace. Malgré son caractère intimiste – avec seulement 44 bungalows –, l'établissement dispose d'un terrain de golf homologué, de terrains d'équitation, de courts de tennis, d'équipements aquatiques, d'un centre de remise en forme, ainsi que d'aménagements halieutiques sur les rives du Rio de la Plata.

SOIN PHARE : TRAITEMENT CORPOREL AU VIN ET À LA SOIE

Four Seasons Resort Carmelo
Ruta 21, Km 262
Carmelo, Dpto. de Colonia
Uruguay

TEL: +598 5429000
FAX: +598 5429999
EMAIL: world.reservations@fourseasons.com
WEBSITE: www.fourseasons.com/carmelo

Bulgari Hotel
Photographs by Reto Guntli/zapaimages

Grotta Giusti Spa & Hotel
Photographs courtesy Grotta Giusti Spa & Hotel

Les Thermes Marins de Monte-Carlo
Architect: Rue and Lionel Bureau
Photos courtesy Les Thermes Marins de Monte-Carlo

Sturebadet
Interior Architect: Hjalmar Molin
Photographs courtesy Stockholms Badhus

Victoria-Jungfrau Grand Hotel & Spa
Photographs by Bruno Helbling/zapaimages

Lenkerhof Alpine Resort
Photographs by Bruno Helbling/zapaimages

Therme Vals
Architect: Peter Zumthor
Photographs by Agi Simões/zapaimages (pp. 164–167, 168–169) and H. P. Schultz (pp. 170–171)

Çemberlitaş
Architect: Mimar Sitan
Photographs Pascal Meunier, Panos Pictures

Harrogate Turkish Baths & Health Spa
Architect: Frank Bagally and Fred Bristowe (1897)
Photographs courtesy Harrogate Turkish Baths & Health Spa

Pages 180–181:
Photograph courtesy of the Four Seasons Hualalai

Willow Stream at the Fairmont Banff Springs
Architect: Bruce Price
Photographs courtesy Fairmont Hotels & Resorts

King Pacific Lodge
Photographs courtesy Rosewood Hotels & Resorts

Sanctuary on Camelback Mountain
Architect: Marc Philip
Interior Designer: Judith Testani
Photographs courtesy Sanctuary at Camelback Mountain

Calistoga Ranch
Photographs by Bryan Burkhart

Sagewater Spa
Architect/Designers: Rhoni Epstein, Cristina Pestana
Photographs by Marcelo Coelho

The Golden Door
Photographs courtesy The Golden Door

Hotel Healdsburg
Architect: David Baker and Partners
Photographs by Cesar Rubio

The Carneros Inn
Architect: William Rawn & Associates
Photographs courtesy The Carneros Inn

Ojai Valley Inn & Spa
Architect: Wallace Neff
Photographs courtesy Ojai Valley Inn & Spa

Viceroy Palm Springs
Interior Designer: Kelly Wearstler
Photographs by Grey Crawford

The Spa du Soleil at the Auberge du Soleil
Architect: Walker & Moody Architects
Photographs by Terence Ford

Tru
Architect/Designer: New World Design Builders/ Chris Kofitsas
Photographs by Eric Laignel

Kenwood Inn + Spa
Architects: Terry and Roseann Grimm
Photographs by James Garrahan

International Orange
Architect: Philip Banta & Associates
Photographs courtesy International Orange

Agua at the Delano Hotel
Architect: PMG Architects
Interior Designer: Philippe Starck
Photographs by Eric Laignel

Château Élan Spa
Interior Designer: Nancy Panoz
Photographs courtesy Château Élan

The Kahala Hotel & Resort
Designer: Henricksen Design Associates
Photographs courtesy Mandarin Oriental

Spa Halekulani
Interior Design: Philpotts & Associates
Photographs courtesy the Halekulani

Four Seasons Resort Hualalai at Historic Ka'upulehu
Photographs courtesy the Four Seasons Hotels & Resorts

The Fairmont Orchid
Photographs courtesy the Fairmont Hotels & Resorts

Four Seasons Resort Maui at Wailea
Architect: Island Design Center
Photographs courtesy the Four Seasons Hotels & Resorts

Ten Thousand Waves
Architect/Interior Designer: Duke Klauck (owner)
Photographs by D. Fleig

Clay
Architect/Interior Designer: Studios Architecture
Photographs by Eric Laignel

The Kiawah Island Club's Sasanqua
Interior Designer: Clodagh
Photographs by Daniel Aubry

The Spa at Sundance
Architect/Interior Designer: Joyce Popendorf
Photographs by Susan Spaeth

Amangani
Architect/Interior Designer: Edward Tuttle
Photographs courtesy Aman Resorts

Pages 288–289:
Photograph by Michael Plumridge

Bedarra Island
Architect: Pike Withers
Photographs courtesy P & O Australian Resorts

Daintree Eco Lodge & Spa
Architect/Interior Designer: Hans & Jan Eyeman
Photographs courtesy Daintree Eco Lodge & Spa

Namale
Architect/Interior Designer: Vitti Architecture
Photographs by Michael Plumridge

Bora Bora Lagoon Resort
Architect/Interior Designer: Fracois Jaulin
Photographs courtesy Bora Bora Lagoon Resort

Pages 306–307:
Photograph courtesy Maroma Resort & Spa

Esperanza
Architects: Backen/Gillam Architects;
Mario Maldonado of GV Arquitectos
Designers: Chhada Siembieda Remedios, Inc.
Photographs courtesy Esperanza

Las Ventanas al Paraíso
Designer: Wilson & Associates
Photographs courtesy Las Ventanas al Paraíso

Hotelito Desconocido
Owner /Developer: Marcello Murzilli
Photographs courtesy Hotelito Desconocido

Maroma Resort & Spa
Architect/Interior Designer: Jaque Robertson, Chris Britton, Graham Viney
Photographs courtesy Venice Simplon-Orient-Express, Ltd.

Verana
Architect/Interior Designer: Heinz Legler and Veronique Lievre
Photographs by Jae Fineberg

Explora en Patagonia
Architect: German del Sol
Photographs courtesy Explora Hotels (pp. 330–333) and Tuca Reinés (pp. 334–337)

Explora en Atacama
Architect: German del Sol
Photographs by Tuca Reinés

Four Seasons Resort Carmelo
Photographs of the Four Seasons Hotels & Resorts

Page 348:
Photograph courtesy Stockholms Badhus

Page 350:
The Bath in Plummers, 1559
Photograph courtesy picture alliance/akg-images

349

Authors & Contributors

Allison Arieff is the Editor in Chief of Dwell, and was the magazine's founding Senior Editor. She is the co-author of Prefab and Trailer Travel: A Visual History of Mobile America, and the editor of numerous books on art and culture including Airstream: The History of the Land Yacht, Hatch Show Print: The History of A Great American Poster Shop, and Cheap Hotels.

Bryan Burkhart is the Creative Director of the design firm Modernhouse. He is the designer and co-author of the books Airstream: The History of the Land Yacht, Prefab, and Trailer Travel: A Visual History of Mobile America, and the designer of the book Cheap Hotels. Burkhart has done design work for companies such as Apple, Sony, Taschen, Chronicle Books, Dwell magazine, and Meta Design. Allison Arieff and Bryan Burkhart live in San Francisco.

Adrienne Arieff is the Director of Arieff Communications, a consumer public relations and branding firm in San Francisco, California. She writes a spa column for Empire Magazine in New York City and can often be found trying exotic spa treatments around the globe.

A contributing editor to Dwell magazine, Deborah Bishop is the author of StyleCity San Francisco (Thames & Hudson) and Hello Midnight: An Insomniac's Literary Bedside Companion (Simon & Schuster). She lives in San Francisco.

Irene Ricasio Edwards, a former editor at Condé Nast Traveler and ONE Media, is the executive editor of 7x7 magazine in San Francisco. Having grown up in Manila, Milan, and New York, she is a fanatical world traveler and takes her passport everywhere she goes.

Autoren & Mitarbeiter

Allison Arieff ist Mitbegründerin und Chefredakteurin des Magazins „Dwell". Sie hat an den Büchern „Prefab" und „Trailer Travel: A Visual History of Mobile America" mitgeschrieben und zahlreiche Bücher über Kunst und Kultur herausgegeben, darunter auch die Titel „Airstream: The History of the Land Yacht", „Hatch Show Print: The History of A Great American Poster Shop" und „Cheap Hotels".

Bryan Burkhart ist Creative Director des Designerbüros Modernhouse. Er war Layouter und Koautor der Bücher „Airstream: The History of the Land Yacht", „Prefab" und „Trailer Travel: A Visual History of Mobile America". Außerdem hat er den Titel „Cheap Hotels" gestaltet. Zu Burkharts Kunden zählen Firmen wie Apple, Sony, Taschen, Chronicle Books, Dwell magazine und Meta Design. Allison Arieff und Bryan Burkhart leben in San Francisco.

Adrienne Arieff ist die Geschäftsführerin von Arieff Communications, einer PR-Firma in San Francisco, Kalifornien. Außerdem verfasst sie eine regelmäßige Spa-Kolumne für die New Yorker Zeitschrift Empire und ist häufig unterwegs, um neue Spa-Behandlungen in aller Welt auszutesten.

Deborah Bishop ist Redakteurin der Zeitschrift „Dwell" und Autorin der Bücher „StyleCity San Francisco" (Thames & Hudson) und „Hello Midnight: An Insomniac's Literary Bedside Companion" (Simon & Schuster). Sie lebt in San Francisco.

Irene Ricasio Edwards, früher Redakteurin bei „Condé Nast Traveler" und „ONE Media" ist Redaktionsleiterin bei dem in San Francisco erscheinenden Magazin „7x7". Edwards, die in Manila, Mailand und New York aufwuchs, ist eine begeisterte Globetrotterin und unternimmt keinen Schritt ohne ihren Pass.

Les Auteurs & Contributions

Allison Arieff est fondatrice et rédactrice en chef du magazine Dwell. Elle a coécrit Prefab et Trailer Travel: A Visual History of Mobile America et publié de nombreux livres sur l'art et la culture, dont Airstream: The History of the Land Yacht, Hatch Show Print: The History of A Great American Poster Shop et Cheap Hotels.

Bryan Burkhart est le directeur artistique de la société de design Moderhouse. Il a conçu et coécrit Airstream: The History of the Land Yacht, Prefab, et Trailer Travel: A Visual History of Mobile America. On lui doit également la conception graphique de Cheap Hotels. Il a travaillé entre autres pour le magazine Dwell, Meta Design, Apple, Sony, Taschen et Chronicle Books. Allison Arieff et Bryan Burkhart vivent à San Francisco.

Adrienne Arieff est directrice de Arieff Communications, une société de relations publiques et de branding basée à San Francisco. Elle tient une chronique sur les spas dans Empire Magazine, et voyage dans le monde entier pour découvrir de nouveaux spas.

Journaliste à Dwell, Deborah Bishop a écrit StyleCity San Francisco (Thames & Hudson), et Hello Midnight: An Insomniac's Literary Bedside Companion (Simon & Schuster). Elle vit à San Francisco.

Irene Ricasio Edwards, ancienne directrice de la publication chez Condée Nast Traveler et chez ONE Media, est aujourd'hui directrice au magazine 7x7. Elle a grandit à Manille, à Milan et à New York – et ne se sépare jamais de son passeport.